T0285856

VEGAN
Barbecue

VEGAN
Barbecue

*More Than
100 Recipes for
Smoky & Satisfying
Plant-Based BBQ*

TERRY SARGENT

HARVARD
COMMON
PRESS

Inspiring | Educating | Creating | Entertaining

Brimming with creative inspiration, how-to projects, and useful information to enrich your everyday life, quarto.com is a favorite destination for those pursuing their interests and passions.

First Published in 2023 by The Harvard Common Press, an imprint of The Quarto Group,
100 Cummings Center, Suite 265-D, Beverly, MA 01915, USA.
T (978) 282-9590 F (978) 283-2742 Quarto.com

The Harvard Common Press titles are also available at discount for retail, wholesale, promotional, and bulk purchase. For details, contact the Special Sales Manager by email at specialsales@quarto.com or by mail at The Quarto Group, Attn: Special Sales Manager, 100 Cummings Center, Suite 265-D, Beverly, MA 01915, USA.

27 26 25 24 23   1 2 3 4 5

ISBN: 978-0-7603-7789-5

Digital edition published in 2022
eISBN: 978-0-7603-7790-1

Library of Congress Cataloging-in-Publication Data

Names: Sargent, Terry, author.
Title: Vegan barbecue : More than 100 recipes for smoky and satisfying plant-based BBQ / Terry Sargent.
Description: Beverly, MA : The Harvard Common Press, 2023. | "Digital edition published in 2022"--T.p. verso. | Summary: "Vegan Barbecue reveals that genuine smoke-cooked BBQ is not just for meats in 100 plant-based recipes for veggies, fruits, and vegan meats and cheeses"--Provided by publisher.
Identifiers: LCCN 2022046505 | ISBN 9780760377895 (trade paperback) | ISBN 9780760377901 (ebook)
Subjects: LCSH: Vegan cooking. | Barbecuing. | Smoking (Cooking) | LCGFT: Cookbooks.
Classification: LCC TX837 .S26533 2023 | DDC 641.5/6362--dc23/eng/20221007
LC record available at https://lccn.loc.gov/2022046505

Design: Tanya Jacobson, tanyajacobson.co
Photography: Bites and Bevs Media, Madeylynne Boykin & Ryan Aaron

Printed in China

*I dedicate this book
to my close friends, family, and the vegan community.
Thank you for your continuous support.*

Contents

Introduction: My Story

There are three things you can count on growing up in the U.S. South. It's going to be hot! It's going to be humid! And somebody's going to have a fire going!

I grew up just north of Atlanta in a town called Roswell. In Roswell we had a blend of cultures that provided a front-row seat to what life would be like once we would reach adulthood. We weren't necessarily poor; we just didn't understand any other way.

Food was always a part of my life. But I didn't know when I was young that it would be something that would take me beyond the streets of Roswell. My first cooking job was—ironically, given where I eventually ended up—cooking steaks on a gas grill at a Texas Roadhouse chain restaurant. I discovered there was just something I loved about the heat and the rush, about having a restaurant full of people and being in control of how a person's meal would go. It was a RUSH!

Once hooked, I began to work my way slowly through the Atlanta restaurant circuit, eventually cooking at some of the top restaurants the city has to offer. The experiences I have taken from these places and the relationships I developed over the years have truly shaped my culinary career.

My final stop was working as a corporate chef for a big-name company. It was one of the easiest jobs I've ever had. Unfortunately, it wasn't challenging. It did not provide that *rush* that had initially christened me into the restaurant industry.

Around this time, I adopted a vegan lifestyle, mainly due to some health issues I had. I quickly came to love the challenge of taking amazing classical dishes and creating vegan versions of them. When I first started, Beyond Meat, Impossible Burger, and other "vegan meat" makers were not yet around and their rumored arrival was just beginning to be talked about. I was not really a tofu fan. So, in my down time outside my boring job, I began to create my own mock meats and to craft vegan dishes that featured them.

I was sitting down one June day in 2019 with one of my dear friends and we began to discuss the lack of good vegan foods available for the upcoming Fourth of July holiday. We were tired of grocery-store frozen vegan burgers and the various brands of crappy vegan hot dogs. I came up with the idea of doing a small popup event geared around vegan BBQ items.

I reached out to a friend, one of my connections in the Atlanta restaurant world, to ask if she would allow me to use her kitchen to prep the food for this popup.

She said yes, and so, on July 4, 2019, we hosted the "VBQ Fest" popup, the official beginning of my vegan barbecue journey.

That first popup event lasted all of 45 minutes, due to the fact we had a line about half a mile long and quickly sold out of every single item we had in house. It was a holiday. People were off of work and looking for something fun to do. It was easy to draw a crowd.

Buoyed by that first success, I thought, "Let's do it again and see if it works." So, the following weekend we did an encore, and we achieved the very same result. From that moment the wheels were turning in my mind, and I was already planning my exit speech from corporate America.

I set up my first non-popup shop later in 2019 in a building that had six other small restaurants, mostly Asian ones, inside it. I decorated my 5-foot-by-5-foot stall and I called it Grass VBQ Joint. Eventually the lease ran up, so we transitioned to a popular local brewery, where we set up inside and served. And then ... COVID! It was the spring of 2020 and the country—the restaurant industry especially—was in shambles, and I had just quit my cushy corporate job to venture out on my own with a new business. Perfect timing, right?

Fortunately, however, we had an excellent location and a robust pick-up and delivery business model that was largely pandemic-proof. So we survived. In fact, sales were strong enough to grant me the ability to open my own standalone brick and mortar restaurant.

Within two years I had one of the very first vegan BBQ restaurants in the country! I was able to establish quite a name for the business, with a lot of positive reviews and even feature articles in the media, and I went on to open a second location.

"Why vegan BBQ?" is a question I am often asked. Actually, the only question I ever asked myself was, "*Why not?*" The main answer is that there was a need. Barbecue cooking and flavoring are essential in the South, but there was no good way for vegans—full-time vegans or part-time ones—to savor and enjoy it. It was a market that had not been tapped yet and I was excited that, for now at least, it was all mine!

The other question I am often asked, naturally enough, is "How do you make vegan BBQ?!" I've answered that million-dollar question, oh, 16,000 times—

and the fact that I am asked so often is why I wrote this book! The definition of barbecue is simple: cooking over an open flame or other heat source, whether in a dedicated smoker or another device, in such a way that the smoke from the flame infuses the food with flavor. That's it! If you can cook it over a smoky open flame, it's BBQ!

In my popups, in restaurants, and in this book, at the heart of my recipes is an insistence on cooking from scratch, without using highly processed shortcut ingredients, and on cooking with authenticity—seeking the true flavors and textures of real barbecue. What does beef taste like? Well, not much until you add something to it—and most of the time what you're adding is a vegan element. So, my biggest challenge was never flavor, it was texture! I had to experiment, and test and retest, to approximate the texture of beef, what it feels like in your mouth, or even in your hand. And I worked hard on other non-vegan ingredients, like cheese. When I developed the best vegan cheese sauce for our smoked mac 'n' cheese, the experience, honestly, felt like it was pure science.

Once I had captured the flavors and textures I was seeking, I felt I couldn't lose: Vegan BBQ could be every bit as good as non-vegan BBQ, and I knew how to cook it just right. Hundreds of hours deep in the trials and errors of mock-meat-making have brought me to where I am today.

Let's get one thing understood. This was *never* the plan. I swore I would never open my own restaurant, due to the fact that I had worked in so many and understood the insane work that goes into running a successful one. But in reality, opening my own restaurant was just something that came easily to me, so much so that I felt I had no choice but to step right into it. To be honest, I feel like I was chosen for this role. Being the chef who would bring vegan BBQ to the forefront of the food scene was a make or break situation—for it surely could have been a disaster. Yet three years after I embarked on this path, I have multiple locations, national recognition, and awards. And, oh yeah, a cookbook! I hope that this book brings you as much joy as you read and cook from it as it brought to me while writing it.

1

Spices, Rubs, Sauces, Salsas, and Marinades

Signature VBQ Spice Rub

I put this stuff on… everything! There's nothing more universal than a good spice rub. This rub literally tastes great on vegetables, mock meats, even juicy fruits! It is guaranteed to be a stable in the spice cabinet.

Combine the brown sugar, smoked paprika, black pepper, smoked salt, ancho chile powder, granulated garlic, granulated onion, cayenne pepper, and stout beer powder, if using, in a medium in a mixing bowl and whisk together. A wire whisk works best to incorporate air and remove lumps. Store in an airtight container at room termpature or keep in the freezer in a sealed zippered bag for up to 3 months.

MAKES ABOUT 1¼ CUPS (210 G)

½ cup (110 g) packed light brown sugar

½ cup (55 g) smoked paprika

1 tablespoon (20 g) freshly ground black pepper

1 tablespoon (20 g) smoked kosher salt

1 tablespoon (20 g) ancho chile powder

1 tablespoon (20 g) granulated garlic

1 tablespoon (20 g) granulated onion

1 teaspoon cayenne pepper

1 teaspoon stout beer powder (optional, may be hard to find)

A Bundle of Flavored Salts

These salts can add that extra flavor burst you need for your savory or sweet dishes. Coarse kosher salt works best with these recipes. Iodized table salt will actually sweat and result in clumpy infused salt.

Sriracha Salt

Try Sriracha Salt on avocado toast, guacamole, roasted vegetables, French fries, grilled fish, mango, pineapple, and watermelon.

Mix together the sriracha sauce and salt in a small bowl. Spread out evenly on a dinner plate. Microwave at 1 minute intervals for 5 minutes, stirring after every minute with a fork. The salt mixture will continue to dry as it cooks. Stir and fluff with a fork. Let cool and dry for several hours on the counter, or overnight. Store in an airtight container at room temperature for up to 1 week.

MAKES ABOUT ¾ CUP (230 G)

⅓ cup (80 ml) sriracha sauce

½ cup (150 g) kosher salt

Mustard Salt

When you need salt with a kick.

Mix together the mustard and salt in a small bowl. Spread evenly on a dinner plate and microwave at 1 minute intervals for 5 minutes, stirring after every minute with a fork. The salt will be slightly damp and will continue to dry as it cooks. Stir and fluff with a fork. Let it cool and dry for several hours on the counter, or overnight. Store in an airtight container at room temperature for up to 1 week.

MAKES ABOUT ¾ CUP (210 G)

⅓ cup (60 g) Dijon mustard

½ cup (150 g) kosher salt

Pinot Noir Salt

If you do not have Pinot Noir on hand, substitute another red wine that you like.

Mix together the wine and salt in a small bowl. Spread evenly on a dinner plate and microwave at 1 minute intervals for 5 minutes, stirring after every minute with a fork. The mixture will be slightly damp and will continue to dry as it cooks. Stir and fluff with a fork. Let the salt air dry for 2 days on the counter. Store in an airtight container at room temperature for up to 1 week.

MAKES ABOUT 1½ CUPS (405 G)

7 tablespoons (105 ml) Pinot Noir

1 cup (300 g) kosher salt

Celery Salt

I never throw out my celery leaves. Here is one of the ways I use them.

Mix together the celery leaves, celery seeds, and salt in a small bowl. Spread evenly on a dinner plate and microwave at 1 minute intervals for 5 minutes, stirring after every minute with a fork. The mixture will be slightly damp and will continue to dry as it cooks. Stir and fluff with a fork. Let the salt air dry for a few hours or overnight on the counter. Store in an airtight container at room temperature for up to 1 week.

MAKES ABOUT 1 CUP (180 G)

½ cup (30 g) very finely chopped celery leaves

1 teaspoon celery seeds

½ cup (150 g) kosher salt

House Seasoning

Outside of desserts, there's almost nothing this simple mix will not enhance.

Mix together the salt, cracked pepper, and granulated garlic in a small bowl. Store in an airtight container at room temperature for up to a month.

MAKES ABOUT 3 CUPS (800 G)

2 cups (600 g) kosher salt

½ cup (120 ml) cracked black pepper

½ cup (80 g) granulated garlic

Infused Olive Oil Trio

I love infused oils! They are great dish finishes and great by themselves with crusty bread.

You can substitute other oils, such as walnut, grapeseed, or almond oil, for the olive oil. Blended vegetable oils and canola oil will not work well because they don't hold flavor well. They are meant for neutral-tasting frying.

Rosemary, Garlic and Chile-Infused Olive Oil

Feel free to jack up the heat level, or temper it down, by using more or fewer chiles.

1   Combine the rosemary, peppercorns, garlic, chiles, salt, and olive oil in a saucepan over low heat. Warm slowly until the mixture starts to gently bubble, 5 to 8 minutes. Continue to heat until the oil is very fragrant, another 1 or 2 minutes.

2   Cool completely, then strain out the solids and pour the oil into a clean bottle to store. Refrigerate and use within a month.

MAKES ABOUT 1 CUP (235 ML)

½ cup (15 g) rosemary sprigs

1 tablespoon (5 g) whole peppercorns

4 cloves garlic, lightly crushed

2 serrano chiles or small dried chipotle chiles or a pinch or two of red pepper flakes

Pinch of kosher salt

1 cup (235 ml) extra-virgin olive oil

Ginger, Star Anise, and Chile-Infused Olive Oil

My go-to infused oil when I want an Asian flavor profile.

1   Combine the ginger, star anise, garlic, chiles, salt, and olive oil in a saucepan over low heat. Warm slowly until the mixture starts to gently bubble, 5 to 8 minutes. Continue to heat until the oil is very fragrant, another 1 or 2 minutes.

2   Cool completely, then strain out the solids and pour the oil into a clean bottle to store. Refrigerate and use within a month.

MAKES ABOUT 1 CUP (235 ML)

¼ cup (25 g) fresh ginger slices

6 star anise

4 cloves garlic, lightly crushed

3 dried bird's eye chiles or other small dried chiles or a pinch or two of red pepper flakes

Pinch of kosher salt

1 cup (235 ml) extra-virgin olive oil

Bay Leaf, Citrus, and Black Peppercorn-Infused Olive Oil

Pretty good, too, with lemon or lime zest instead of orange, but I always return to orange.

1   Combine the bay leaves, orange zest, peppercorns, salt, and olive oil in a saucepan over low heat. Warm slowly until the mixture starts to gently bubble, 5 to 8 minutes. Continue to heat until the oil is very fragrant, another 1 or 2 minutes.

2   Cool completely, then strain out the solids and pour the oil into a clean bottle to store. Refrigerate and use within a month.

MAKES ABOUT 1 CUP (235 ML)

¼ cup (10 g) dried bay leaves

Zest of 1 orange (no pith)

1 tablespoon (5 g) whole black peppercorns

Pinch of kosher salt

1 cup (235 ml) extra-virgin olive oil

Citrus Potato Dust

This dust never settles. This seasoning can be used for anything — not just potatoes, where it really shines — and even on fruit! It's the perfect balance of sour and sweet, earthiness and freshness.

Combine the lemon zest, orange zest, coriander, and pepper in a small airtight container. Cover and shake well to combine. To store, refrigerate for up to 1 week.

MAKES ABOUT ½ CUP (50 G)

8 teaspoons (15 g) finely grated lemon zest (from 2 lemons)

¼ cup (25 g) finely grated orange zest (from 2 oranges)

4 teaspoons (5 g) ground coriander

2 teaspoons (5 g) freshly ground black pepper

Roasted Garlic Smoked Butta

Fat is flavor, and this recipe provides a full load of flavor. This smoked butter can be used in any dish. You can even sear and sauté in it. My favorite plant-based butter to use for this recipe is Miyoko Brand.

MAKES ¾ CUP (175 ML)

½ cup (110 g) unsalted vegan butter

1 head garlic

1 teaspoon extra-virgin olive oil

2 tablespoons (8 g) chopped fresh herbs, such as parsley, rosemary, thyme, or chives

¼ teaspoon kosher salt (optional)

1   Remove the butter from the refrigerator and allow to come to room temperature. Meanwhile, preheat the oven to 400°F (200°C).

2   Remove the excess peels from the outside of the garlic head. Slice off and discard ¼ inch (5 mm) from the wide/root end to expose the cloves. Make a little bowl of foil to set the head of garlic in, which will help hold the garlic cloves together and upright. Drizzle the olive oil over the garlic, then cover completely with foil. Roast in the oven for 40 to 50 minutes, until the garlic is soft throughout and lightly browned. Remove from the oven and allow to cool before handling.

3   Peel the garlic. Combine the garlic, vegan butter, fresh herbs, and salt in a food processor. Blend until the ingredients are evenly incorporated.

4   Using waxed paper, form the butter into a log and wrap tightly. Refrigerate until chilled. Slice and serve as needed, storing leftovers in the refrigerator. This compound butter will keep for 1 to 2 weeks in a sealed container in the refrigerator, or for up to 6 months in the freezer.

"Bacun" Marinade

Can be used for marinating vegetables.

Combine the tamari, maple syrup, paprika, tomato paste, granulated garlic, granulated onion, and liquid smoke in jar or bowl. Shake or whisk together. Use immediately or store for up to 1 week in the refrigerator.

MAKES ABOUT ⅓ CUP (80 ML)

2 tablespoons (30 ml) tamari

2 tablespoons (30 ml) pure maple syrup

1 teaspoon smoked paprika

1 tablespoon (15 g) tomato paste

¼ teaspoon granulated garlic

¼ teaspoon granulated onion

⅛ teaspoon liquid smoke

VBQ Mediterranean Marinade

Pickles pickles pickles! Sweet, tangy, spicy! Pickles are a labor of love.

Combine the canola oil, balsamic vinegar, garlic, parsley, basil, red pepper flakes, Italian seasoning, salt, and pepper in a jar or bowl. Shake or whisk together. Use immediately or store for up to 1 week in the refrigerator.

MAKES ABOUT ⅔ CUP (160 ML)

¼ cup (60 ml) canola oil

¼ cup (60 ml) balsamic vinegar

2 teaspoons (5 g) minced garlic

1 tablespoon (5 g) minced fresh flat-leaf parsley

1 tablespoon (5 g) minced fresh basil

½ teaspoon red pepper flakes

2½ tablespoons (10 g) Italian seasoning

½ teaspoon kosher salt

½ teaspoon freshly ground black pepper

Kickin' Jerk Marinade

This jerk sauce comes straight from the islands. The Scotch bonnet provides that level of heat and flavor to make you think you're really there under the sun.

Combine the Scotch bonnets, red onion, garlic, scallions, soy sauce, cider vinegar, olive oil, orange juice, lime juice, ginger, brown sugar, nutmeg, allspice, cinnamon, thyme, salt, and pepper in a food processor. Process until smooth. Use immediately to marinate.

Note   You can always replace the Scotch bonnets with a milder chile, such as jalapeño.

MAKES ABOUT 2 CUPS (475 ML)

4 to 6 Scotch bonnet peppers, chopped

1 small red onion, chopped

4 to 6 cloves garlic, chopped

4 scallions, green and white parts

¼ cup (60 ml) soy sauce

¼ cup (60 ml) apple cider vinegar

2 tablespoons (30 ml) extra-virgin olive oil

¾ cup (90 ml) fresh orange juice

Juice from half a lime

1 tablespoon (10 g) freshly grated ginger

2 tablespoons (30 g) packed light brown sugar

1 teaspoon ground nutmeg

1 teaspoon ground allspice

1 teaspoon ground cinnamon

1 teaspoon dried thyme

Kosher salt and freshly ground black pepper

Sneaky Cocoa Faux Meat Rub

Cocoa has a way of adding just a light touch of sweet to most savory recipes. Paired with an assortment of spices, this rub will hit on all of your flavor notes. The better the quality of cocoa, the better your rub will be.

Combine the cocoa, brown sugar, paprika, salt, chili powder, granulated garlic, granulated onion, and cinnamon in an airtight container. Whisk or shake to combine. Store at room temperature for up to 1 month.

MAKES ABOUT 1¼ CUPS (200 G)

⅓ cup (30 g) unsweetened cocoa powder

½ cup (110 g) packed light brown sugar

2 tablespoons (10 g) smoked paprika

2 tablespoons (20 g) kosher salt

1 tablespoon (10 g) chili powder

1 tablespoon (10 g) granulated garlic

1 tablespoon (10 g) granulated onion

½ teaspoon ground cinnamon

Vegan Bacon Jalapeño Fry Sauce

If you've tried this recipe, come back and let us know how it was in the comments or star ratings!

Combine the ketchup, vegan mayonnaise, pickled jalapeños, mustard, cider vinegar, pepper, and sugar in a bowl or food processor. Blitz or whisk until combined. Fold in the bacon by hand. Cover and chill the sauce for at least an hour before serving.

MAKES ABOUT 1½ CUPS (355 ML)

½ cup (120 g) ketchup

½ cup (110 g) vegan mayonnaise

2 tablespoons (20 g) minced pickled jalapeños

1 teaspoon yellow mustard

1 teaspoon apple cider vinegar

½ teaspoon freshly ground black pepper

½ teaspoon sugar

1 strip vegan bacon

VBQ Chimichurri Sauce

Chimichurri has a very European flavor profile, but its origins are in Argentina and Uruguay.

1   Heat the olive oil in a medium saucepan over medium heat. Add the bell pepper, carrot, scallions, onion, celery, and garlic and cook until softened but not brown, about 5 minutes.

2   Stir in the parsley, capers, tomato sauce, water, tomato paste, cider vinegar, and oregano. Season with salt and black pepper to taste and cook, uncovered, until thick and fragrant, about 10 minutes.

3   Transfer the sauce to a food processor or blender and process to a puree, then return it to the pan and cook over medium-low heat for 5 minutes. Remove the chimichurri from the heat and taste for seasoning, adding more cider vinegar and/or salt as necessary; the sauce should be highly seasoned.

4   Transfer the chimichurri to a serving bowl and serve hot or at room temperature. The sauce can be stored, tightly covered in the refrigerator, for at least 3 days.

MAKES ABOUT 4 CUPS (950 ML)

½ cup (120 ml) extra-virgin olive oil

½ medium red bell pepper, seeded and diced

½ medium carrot, diced

2 scallions, both white and green parts, diced

¼ medium onion, diced

1 medium rib celery, diced

1 clove garlic, finely chopped

2 tablespoons (10 g) chopped fresh flat-leaf parsley

2 teaspoons drained capers

1 cup (240 ml) tomato sauce

½ cup (120 ml) water

¼ cup (65 g) tomato paste

1 tablespoon (15 ml) apple cider vinegar, or more to taste

1 teaspoon dried oregano

Kosher salt and lots of freshly ground black pepper

Alabama White VBQ Sauce

Traditionally a mayo-based sauce, this vegan version has a bit of a kick but still an underline of sweetness. Pairs great with any vegan dish.

Combine the vegan mayonnaise, cider vinegar, horseradish, sugar, lemon juice, mustard, paprika, and salt in a bowl and whisk until completely combined. Serve immediately or cover and store in the fridge for up to 5 days.

MAKES ABOUT 1½ CUPS
(355 ML)

1 cup (225 g) vegan mayonnaise

1½ tablespoons (25 ml) apple cider vinegar

4 teaspoons (20 g) prepared horseradish

2 teaspoons sugar

2 teaspoons (10 ml) fresh lemon juice

1 teaspoon Dijon mustard

¼ teaspoon smoked paprika

½ teaspoon kosher salt

Moppin' Sauce

Moppin' sauce is generally used to increase the flavor of your grilled items and items in the smoker. This version is good for all kinds of plant-based meats, as well as vegetables, during the grilling process.

1 Combine the cider vinegar, water, brown sugar, salt, black pepper, cayenne, and red pepper flakes in a saucepan over medium heat. Stir until the salt dissolves and the sauce is hot.

2 Cool and set aside 2 cups (480 ml) for serving; use the rest for mopping vegan meat and vegetables as they cook. Extra can be refrigerated in an airtight container for up to 3 months. Stir before using.

MAKES ABOUT 5 CUPS (1 L)

4½ cups (1 L) apple cider vinegar

¾ cup (175 ml) water

2 tablespoons (30 g) packed light brown sugar

1 teaspoon kosher salt

1 teaspoon freshly ground black pepper

½ teaspoon cayenne pepper

½ teaspoon red pepper flakes

Smackin' Creole VBQ Sauce

My version of this Southern classic. I'm a big fan of vinegar-based sauces, and this one hits perfectly.

Combine the cider vinegar, brown sugar, and salt in a medium saucepan and bring to a boil. Add the salt, granulated garlic, granulated onion, black pepper, red pepper flakes, hot sauce, and ketchup. Simmer over low heat for 15 minutes. Cool and serve. Store extra in an airtight container in the refrigerator for up to 1 month.

MAKES ABOUT 4 CUPS (945 ML)

3 cups (720 ml) apple cider vinegar

¼ cup (55 g) packed light brown sugar

2 teaspoons kosher salt

2 teaspoons granulated garlic

2 teaspoons granulated onion

½ teaspoon freshly ground black pepper

1 tablespoon (10 g) red pepper flakes

1 teaspoon hot sauce

⅓ cup (70 g) ketchup

Smoky Vidalia VBQ Sauce

Grass VBQ's original barbecue sauce, named for our home state's venerable sweet onion. Invented out of love and still the staple of the GVBQ sauce line.

Heat the oil in a large saucepan over medium heat. Add the onions and cook, stirring often, until translucent, 3 to 5 minutes. Add the ketchup, cider vinegar, honey, lemon juice, Worcestershire, mustard, black pepper, and cayenne. Bring to a boil over high heat. Reduce the heat to maintain a low simmer and cook, stirring occasionally, for 30 minutes. Serve hot or at room temperature. Store extra in an airtight container in the refrigerator for up to 1 month.

MAKES 5 TO 6 CUPS (1 TO 1.4 L)

1 tablespoon (15 ml) canola oil

2 medium sweet onions (about 1 pound/455 g), preferably Vidalia, diced

2½ cups (600 g) ketchup

½ cup (120 ml) apple cider vinegar

¼ cup (85 g) honey

2 tablespoons (30 ml) fresh lemon juice

2 tablespoons (30 ml) vegan Worcestershire sauce

2 tablespoons (20 g) Dijon mustard

½ teaspoon freshly ground black pepper

Pinch of cayenne pepper, or to taste

Sweet Horsey Mustard Sauce

This is my version of a kicked-up honey mustard dipping sauce. I love the unorthodox heat signature of horseradish paired with mustard.

Combine the mustard, honey, brown sugar, cider vinegar, horseradish, ketchup, coconut aminos, and granulated garlic in a medium bowl. Mix well. Refrigerate in an airtight container overnight to allow the flavors to develop. Store extra in the refrigerator for up to 1 month.

MAKES ABOUT 2 CUPS (475 ML)

1 cup (175 g) yellow mustard

¼ cup (85 g) honey

¼ cup (60 g) packed light brown sugar

½ cup (60 ml) apple cider vinegar

1 tablespoon (15 g) prepared horseradish

2 tablespoons (30 g) ketchup

2 teaspoons (10 ml) coconut aminos

1 teaspoon granulated garlic

Freshly ground black pepper

Smoky Creole Remoulade

If you are used to ballpark-style green relish in a jar, give this Creole alternative a spin to liven things up.

Mix together the vegan mayonnaise, mustard, paprika, horseradish, pickle juice, hot sauce, and garlic in a medium bowl. Add 1 teaspoon of the Cajun seasoning and mix together. Taste and add as much of the remaining teaspoon of Creole seasoning, as you like. Chill the remoulade. The remoulade is better if left for a few hours to let the flavors meld. Keep refrigerated.

MAKES ABOUT 2 CUPS (475 ML)

1¼ cups (280 g) vegan mayonnaise

¼ cup (45 g) creole mustard

1 tablespoon (5 g) sweet paprika

2 teaspoons (10 g) prepared horseradish

1 teaspoon sweet pickle juice

1 teaspoon hot sauce

1 large clove garlic, minced and smashed

1 to 2 teaspoons (5 g) Cajun seasoning

Smoked Pineapple Salsa

If your store is out of fresh pineapples, substitute canned pineapple—but drain the sugary syrup before you add the fruit to the salsa.

1 Set up your smoker for 20-minute smoke session over low heat.

2 Brush the pineapple with olive oil and place in the smoker. Smoke for 20 minutes.

3 Set aside to cool.

4 Combine the pineapple, peaches, jalapeño, onion, and lime juice in a medium bowl. Season with salt and garnish with cilantro. Use immediately. Store extra in an airtight container in the refrigerator for up to 1 week.

MAKES 6 TO 8 CUPS (1.4 TO 1.9 L)

1 fresh pineapple, peeled, cored, and chopped into 1-inch (2.5 cm) pieces

Extra-virgin olive oil

2 peaches, pitted and chopped

1 jalapeño, minced

½ red onion, chopped

Juice of 1 lime

Kosher salt

2 tablespoons (2 g) chopped fresh cilantro

Note The longer the salsa sits, the better the flavors. You can reduce the amount of jalapeño for less heat.

Smoked Salsa Trio

Salsa has been known to come in all flavors and varieties. This trio consist of some of my favorite salsas. Tacos beware!!

Traditional Smoked Salsa

The classic pico de gallo mix.

Combine the tomatoes, onion, cilantro, jalapeño, and lime juice in a small bowl. Add salt and pepper to taste and serve.

MAKES ABOUT 1¼ CUPS (295 ML)

2 smoked plum (Roma) tomatoes, chopped

½ cup (80 g) chopped red onion

½ cup (10 g) chopped fresh cilantro

1 jalapeño, seeded and finely chopped

Juice of 1 lime

Kosher salt and freshly ground black pepper

Avocado Salsa

Depending on how chunky you like your salsa, you can chop the ingredients in larger chunks, or you can mince or dice them for a smoother salsa.

Combine the avocado, tomatoes, onion, cilantro, and lime juice in a small bowl. Add salt and pepper to taste and serve.

MAKES ABOUT 1½ CUPS (255 G)

1 avocado, pitted, peeled, and chopped

2 plum (Roma) tomatoes, chopped

¼ cup (40 g) chopped red onion

¼ cup (5 g) chopped fresh cilantro

Juice of 1 lime

Kosher salt and freshly ground black pepper

Mango Salsa

You do not have to smoke the mango, but it's awfully good that way. Smoke the fruit for 15 minutes over low heat.

Combine the mango, onion, cilantro, jalapeño, and lime juice in a medium bowl. Add salt and pepper to taste and serve.

MAKES ABOUT 2 CUPS (475 ML)

1 ripe medium mango, seeded, peeled, chopped, and smoked

½ cup (80 g) chopped red onion

¼ cup (5 g) chopped fresh cilantro

1 jalapeño, seeded and finely chopped

Juice of 1 lime

Kosher salt and freshly ground black pepper

Candied Jalapeño Relish

Who can resist the win-win combination of hot and sweet?

MAKES 12 HALF-PINT
(235 ML) OR 6 PINT
(475 ML) JARS

3 pounds (1.4 kilograms) jalapeños, chopped

2 cups (475 ml) apple cider vinegar

6 cups (1.2 kg) sugar

¼ teaspoon ground turmeric

¼ teaspoon celery seeds

1 tablespoon (10 g) granulated garlic

1 teaspoon ground cayenne pepper

1 Prepare for water bath canning. Gather lids, screwbands, and 12 half-pint (235 ml) and 6 pint (475 ml) mason jars. Inspect the jars for smooth rims. Do not use jars with chipped rims. Fill the water bath canner with water and bring to a boil. Lower the heat and keep at a simmer. Count out jar lids needed for one batch. Set them in water to cover in a bowl.

2 To sterilize jars, wash them in the dishwasher on the sterilize cycle and leave them in to keep them hot while building the recipe. Or put them in a large pot, fill with water to cover, and boil for 10 minutes. Leave in the water.

3 Cut the stems off the jalapeños. Leaving seeds in the peppers, cut the peppers into ¼-inch (5 mm) rounds. (You can seed the peppers if you want a less hot relish, but the heat is surprisingly good in this recipe). Set the peppers aside.

4 Pour the cider vinegar into a large pot. Add the sugar, turmeric, celery seeds, granulated garlic, and cayenne. Stir it all together and bring the syrup to a boil. Lower the heat and simmer for 5 minutes. Add the sliced peppers and simmer for exactly 4 minutes.

5 Use a slotted spoon to transfer the cooked pepper slices to the prepared hot sterilized jars.

6 With a ladle (and canning funnel if you have one), pour the boiling syrup over the peppers to ½ inch (1 cm) from the jar lip. (Do not overfill the jars.)

7 Take a knife or chopstick and insert it into the jar in several places to release trapped air in the pepper/syrup mix. Wipe the jar top with a clean, damp towel (paper towels are easy).

8   Set the lid on each jar top. Secure the lids with screwbands, turned to fingertip tightness.

9   Place the jars in the simmering water in the canner, cover, and bring the water to full rolling boil. Start your timing when the water is at a full rolling boil. Process ½-pint (235 ml) jars for 10 minutes; process pints (475 ml) for 15 minutes. Keep the full boil going until the processing is done. With your canning tongs, remove the hot jars from the canner to a cooling rack (or dry towel on counter).

10 Let the jars sit 24 hours. The seals will complete as the jars cool. You may hear the lids making popping sounds as the lids suck down onto the jars. The jars are sealed when the tiny bump on the lid top sucks down.

11 When the jars are sealed and cooled after 24 hours, remove the screwbands. Label and store the jars in a cool dark cupboard. Let them sit at least 2 weeks (or a month) before opening to allow the flavors to fully develop.

Note   Wear gloves to handle the peppers. Keep your hands away from your face, eyes, lips, and other sensitive parts. The pepper oil is *hot*. Wash your hands after chopping.

Salads

Greens and Apple Salad

A fresh salad for any time of year, but be sure to enjoy it in the fall when apples are at their peak. Apples and feta go especially well together, and they complement a smoked main course nicely.

MAKE THE VINAIGRETTE:

1   Whisk together the olive oil, apple cider vinegar, honey, mustard, and salt in a jar or bowl until well blended. Season to taste with pepper.

MAKE THE SALAD:

2   Toast the pepitas in a medium skillet over medium heat, stirring frequently, until they begin turning golden on the edges, about 60 seconds. Transfer the pepitas to a small bowl to cool.

3   Cut the apple into thin, bite-size slices. Put the greens in a large serving bowl. Top with the apple slices, cranberries, and pepitas. Crumble the vegan feta over the salad.

4   Drizzle the vinaigrette over the salad. Gently toss to mix all of the ingredients well. Serve immediately.

SERVES 4

APPLE CIDER VINAIGRETTE

¼ cup (60 ml) extra-virgin olive oil

1½ tablespoons (25 ml) apple cider vinegar

1½ teaspoons honey or agave syrup

1 teaspoon whole-grain mustard

¼ teaspoon kosher salt

Freshly ground black pepper

SALAD

¼ cup (35 g) pepitas

1 large or 2 small Granny Smith apples

5 ounces (140 g) mixed spring salad greens

⅓ cup (40 g) dried cranberries

⅓ cup (60 g) vegan feta cheese

Smoked Pea Salad

The smoky flavor in this salad comes not from cooking the peas in a smoker but from the crisply cooked tempeh bacon, an essential — and versatile — ingredient in any vegan cook's repertoire.

1   Put the peas in a colander and run them under cool running water to remove any ice. You do not need to thaw them completely at this stage. Drain them well. Combine in a large bowl with the vegan cheese, celery, and red onion.

2   Whisk together the vegan sour cream, vegan mayonnaise, apple cider vinegar, salt, and pepper in a small bowl. Pour this sauce over the peas and stir to mix well. Set the peas aside on your counter while you cook the tempeh bacon.

3   Cook the bacon in a medium pan over medium heat until crispy, about 8 minutes. Set aside to cool to room temperature, then chop in ¼-inch (5-mm) slices. Just before serving, mix the bacon into the peas.

SERVES 4

4 cups (520 g) frozen peas

½ cup (60 g) shredded vegan cheddar cheese

½ cup (60 g) minced celery

⅓ cup (55 g) minced red onion

½ cup (115 g) vegan sour cream

¼ cup (60 g) vegan mayonnaise

1 tablespoon (15 ml) apple cider vinegar

½ teaspoon kosher salt

½ teaspoon freshly ground black pepper

4 slices tempeh bacon (Lightlife Organic Tempeh Strips Smoky Fakin Bacon is recommended)

Roasted Beet and Kale Salad

I know some people who are not the biggest fans of beets, and I know others who do not love kale. But, oddly enough, I haven't encountered anyone who does not like this fresh and crunchy salad combining the two.

1   Preheat the oven to 425°F (220°C). Line a baking sheet with parchment paper.

MAKE THE SALAD:

2   Put the beets on the prepared baking sheet, drizzle the olive oil over them, and use your hands to toss the beets in the oil. Cover the baking sheet with aluminum foil and bake for 30 to 40 minutes, until the beets can be pierced with a fork.

3   While the beets are roasting, prepare the rest of the salad. In a small frying pan over medium-high heat, toast the walnuts until they are fragrant and start to brown in places, 5 to 7 minutes, shaking the pan frequently. Pour the maple syrup over them and sprinkle with the salt and pepper. Continue to cook, stirring constantly, until the maple syrup has almost evaporated, about 1 minute more. Remove the walnuts from the pan and place them on a piece of parchment paper, separating them from each other as much as possible.

MAKE THE DRESSING:

4   Combine the cider vinegar, maple syrup, balsamic vinegar, mustard, garlic, and salt in a medium bowl. Slowly add the oil in a thin steady stream while whisking constantly. If the oil starts to build up at all, stop pouring it and whisk the dressing vigorously. It will take you about 1 minute to whisk in the oil. Taste the dressing, and season to taste with more salt, if needed.

5   Combine the kale and candied walnuts in a large salad bowl. When the beets come out of the oven, let them cool slightly, then add them to the bowl. Pour in the dressing. Toss well so that everything is coated, and serve.

SERVES 4 TO 6

SALAD

1½ pounds (680 g) fresh beets, peeled, quartered, and cut into into bite-size pieces

1 teaspoon extra-virgin olive oil

1 cup (100 g) walnut halves

3 tablespoons (45 ml) pure maple syrup

¼ teaspoon kosher salt

⅛ teaspoon freshly cracked black pepper

4 packed cups (300 g) curly kale, stemmed and torn into bite-size pieces

DRESSING

3 tablespoons (45 ml) apple cider vinegar

2 tablespoons (20 g) pure maple syrup

1 teaspoon balsamic vinegar

½ teaspoon Dijon mustard

1 clove garlic, grated

Pinch of kosher, plus more to taste

¼ cup (60 ml) extra-virgin olive oil

Smoked Macaroni Salad

Kids will try just about anything made with macaroni, right? If you've got a crowd of them on hand, serve up this salad — adjusting the quantities upward as needed. The adults will be happy, too.

MAKE THE SALAD:

1   Combine the macaroni, celery, bell peppers, and onion in a large bowl.

MAKE THE DRESSING:

2   Combine the mayonnaise, apple cider vinegar, mustard, agave, salt, black pepper, cayenne pepper, and liquid smoke in another bowl. Whisk together until well combined.

3   Pour the dressing over the macaroni and vegetables. Mix well until everything is thoroughly coated.

4   Refrigerate for at least 4 hours, and preferably overnight, before serving.

SERVES 4

SALAD

8 ounces (225 g) elbow macaroni, cooked and drained

1 cup (100 g) chopped celery

½ cup (75 g) chopped green bell pepper

½ cup (75 g) chopped red bell pepper

⅓ cup (55 g) chopped red onion

DRESSING

¾ cup (175 g) vegan mayonnaise

2 tablespoons (30 ml) apple cider vinegar

1 tablespoon (10 g) Dijon mustard

1 teaspoon agave syrup

1 teaspoon kosher salt

¼ teaspoon freshly ground black pepper

¼ teaspoon cayenne pepper

½ teaspoon liquid smoke

Rustic Potato Salad

This is a great, nontraditional potato salad. The skin on the potatoes provides a great meaty texture; I like the Red Bliss variety.

MAKE THE SALAD:

1   Combine the sliced potatoes and salt in a large saucepan or Dutch oven. Cover with water by 1 inch (2.5 cm). Bring to a boil over high heat, then reduce the heat to medium-low and cook until the potatoes are easily pierced by a paring knife, 5 to 6 minutes. Reserve ¼ cup (60 ml) of the cooking water, then drain. Transfer the potatoes to a large mixing bowl.

MAKE THE DRESSING:

2   Combine the olive oil, parsley, scallions, lemon juice, mayonnaise, mustard, garlic, and black pepper in a small food processor or blender. Process until the parsley, scallions, and garlic are finely chopped. While running the machine, pour in the reserved cooking water and process just until blended. If you don't have a food processor or blender, just finely chop the parsley and scallions, and whisk together the dressing ingredients until the oil is fully incorporated.

3   Drizzle the potatoes with the olive oil mixture and gently mix to combine. It will look like you've poured in too much dressing, but don't worry, the potatoes will soak it up! Let the potatoes rest for 10 minutes, gently tossing every few minutes.

4   Add the celery to the salad, along with a couple of tablespoons each of parsley and scallions. Toss again. Season to taste generously with salt and pepper.

5   Serve immediately, or cover and refrigerate until you're ready to serve. This salad is best served within a few hours, but it will keep in the refrigerator for 2 to 3 days.

SERVES 6

SALAD

2 pounds (900 g) small red potatoes, skins on, sliced into ¼-inch (5-mm) rounds

1 tablespoon (15 g) kosher salt, plus more to taste

3 stalks celery, chopped

Chopped fresh flat-leaf parsley

Chopped scallions, green and white parts

Freshly ground black pepper

DRESSING

¼ cup (60 ml) extra-virgin olive oil

⅓ cup (20 g) coarsely chopped and lightly packed fresh flat-leaf parsley

⅓ cup (35 g) coarsely chopped scallions, green and white parts

2 tablespoons (30 ml) fresh lemon juice

½ cup (115 g) vegan mayonnaise

2 teaspoons Dijon mustard

2 cloves garlic, coarsely chopped

Freshly ground black pepper

Smoked Mexican Corn Salad

If you are new to smoking vegetables, corn is an easy food to start with: it cooks (smokes) quickly; and your timing does not have to be terribly precise.

SMOKE THE CORN:

1   Preheat a smoker to medium-high heat. Brush the corn with olive oil. Smoke the ears for 20 minutes over low heat. Remove the corn from the smoker and set aside to cool. Once cool, slice the kernels off the ears.

MAKE THE SALAD:

2   Combine the mayonnaise, garlic, and lime zest and juice in a large bowl. Add the corn and scallions and stir to coat. Add the feta, cilantro, smoked paprika, jalapeño, and salt. Season to taste with more salt, it needed.

3   Serve immediately at room temperature, or chill for up to 1 day before serving.

SERVES 4

SMOKED CORN

4 ears fresh corn, shucked

Extra-virgin olive oil, for brushing

SALAD

1½ tablespoons (10 g) vegan mayonnaise

1 clove garlic, minced

Zest and juice of 1 lime

⅓ cup (35 g) chopped scallions, white and green parts

¼ cup (45 g) vegan feta cheese

¼ cup (5 g) finely chopped fresh cilantro

¼ teaspoon smoked paprika

1 jalapeño, diced

¼ teaspoon kosher salt, plus more if needed

Brussels Sprout Salad

The sweetness from the apricots and honey takes the edge off the hint of bitterness that Brussels sprouts have. The walnuts complement the sprouts' nuttiness, and bacon and Brussels sprouts are a timeless pairing.

1   Preheat the oven to 375°F (190°C).

MAKE THE SALAD:

2   Put the walnuts in a small baking dish. Put the tempeh bacon in another small baking dish. Toast both of them in the oven for 10 minutes, or until the walnuts are fragrant and light brown. Remove both baking dishes from the oven. When they are cool enough to handle, coarsely chop the walnuts.

3   Crumble the crisped bacon and combine it with the toasted walnuts, Brussels sprouts, and apricots in a large bowl.

MAKE THE DRESSING:

4   Combine the olive oil, cider vinegar, honey, salt, and pepper in a small bowl and whisk to combine.

5   Pour over the the salad and toss to coat well. Season to taste with salt and pepper and serve immediately.

SERVES 4 TO 6

SALAD

½ cup (50 g) walnut halves

⅓ cup (60 g) chopped tempeh bacon (Lightlife Organic Tempeh Strips Smoky Fakin Bacon is recommended)

3 cups (265 g) shredded or very finely chopped Brussels sprouts

½ cup (65 g) chopped dried apricots

DRESSING

1 tablespoon (15 ml) extra-virgin olive oil

1 tablespoon (15 ml) apple cider vinegar

¼ teaspoon honey

Pinch of kosher salt, plus more to taste

Pinch of freshly ground black pepper, plus more to taste

Smoked Tomato Feta Salad

The fruit that never got its just dues, the tomato is by far one of my favorite things to eat. This salad screams summer and holds up well against the smokiness of feta.

Combine the cucumbers, tomatoes, and red onion in a large bowl. Crumble in the feta cheeze and add the fresh dill. Add the olive oil, salt, and pepper, and mix well. Serve immediately.

SERVES 4

4 cucumbers, finely diced

1 cup (150 g) cherry tomatoes, halved

¼ medium red onion, thinly sliced

½ cup (75 g) Smoked Feta Cheeze (see recipe, page 171)

¼ cup (15 g) chopped fresh dill

1½ tablespoons (25 ml) extra-virgin olive oil

¼ teaspoon kosher salt

¼ teaspoon freshly ground black pepper

Toasted Broccoli Salad

If you cook broccoli in the oven for 40 minutes or so, it is "roasted." Here, half of the broccoli is roasted in the oven for just 20 minutes so it is "toasted"—lightly crispy, but still fresh and not fully cooked through.

1 Preheat the oven to 350°F (175°C).

MAKE THE SALAD:

2 Place a little over half the broccoli on a baking sheet and drizzle it with olive oil. Roast for 20 minutes, or until it starts to brown. At the same time, spread out the pecans in a small baking dish and toast the pecans for 6 to 7 minutes, until fragrant and lightly colored.

3 Cook the tempeh bacon in a frying pan over medium-high heat for 6 to 7 minutes, until crispy. Set aside to cool.

MAKE THE DRESSING:

4 Combine the yogurt, mayonnaise, cider vinegar, salt, pepper, lemon zest, lemon juice, and garlic in a jar with a lid. Cover tightly and shake well.

5 Combine the toasted and raw broccoli in a salad bowl. Add the tempeh bacon, pecans, blueberries, and onion. Top with the dressing, toss well, and serve.

SERVES 4

SALAD

3 small to medium heads broccoli, chopped into ½ inch (1 cm) pieces

Extra-virgin olive oil

1¼ cups (140 g) pecans

1 pound (455 g) tempeh bacon, diced into ½ inch (1 cm) pieces (Lightlife Organic Tempeh Strips Smoky Fakin Bacon is recommended)

2 cups (280 g) frozen blueberries, thawed

¼ cup (30 g) thinly sliced red onion

DRESSING

½ cup (115 g) plain vegan yogurt

¼ cup (60 g) vegan mayonnaise

1 tablespoon (15 ml) apple cider vinegar

½ teaspoon kosher salt

½ teaspoon freshly ground black pepper

Zest and juice of 1 lemon

1 clove garlic

Carolina Red Slaw

This slaw has a more intense flavor than traditional cole slaw.

1   Mix together the cabbage, onion, and carrot in a medium mixing bowl.

2   In a separate bowl, whisk together the ketchup, cider vinegar, sugar, pepper flakes, salt, barbecue seasoning, and hot sauce.

3   Pour the dressing over the slaw and mix well. Taste and adjust the seasoning. Transfer into an airtight container and chill for several hours, or overnight.

SERVES 4

6 cups (420 g) finely chopped green cabbage

¼ cup (40 g) finely chopped red onion

¼ cup (30 g) finely chopped carrot

½ cup (120 ml) ketchup

½ cup (120 ml) apple cider vinegar

3 tablespoons (35 g) sugar

2 teaspoons red pepper flakes, or adjust to taste

1 teaspoon kosher salt

1 teaspoon barbecue seasoning

1 teaspoon hot sauce, or adjust to taste

3

Sandwiches

Tempeh BLT

Tempeh BLTs have a reputation of shining light on extremely talented people. (HEEEY AUNTIE!) At once sweet, smoky, and savory, this sandwich is a can't miss!

SERVES 2

1   Place the sliced tempeh in a baking dish. Whisk together the next 10 ingredients to make a marinade, and pour the marinade over the tempeh. Set the tempeh aside to marinate while you preheat the oven. (You can also cover and store in the refrigerator for up to 24 hours.)

2   Preheat the oven to 350°F (177°C). When the oven is hot, arrange your tempeh in a single layer on a baking sheet or tray. Bake for 15 minutes, flip the tempeh over, and bake for 7 to 10 minutes more, until the tempeh bacon is dark and crisped.

3   To assemble the sandwiches: Slather 2 slices of bread with vegan mayonnaise and the other 2 with Dijon mustard. Layer the lettuce, tomato, and tempeh bacon on one of the mayonnaise slices and top the sandwiches with the mustard slices. If you like, you can toast the sandwiches on a lightly greased hot skillet until the bread is golden. Enjoy!

8 ounces (227 g) tempeh, purchased precut, or thinly sliced by you

2 tablespoons (30 g) liquid aminos

1 tablespoon (15 g) apple cider vinegar

1 tablespoon (15 g) vegetable oil

1 tablespoon (20 g) light agave syrup

½ teaspoon liquid smoke

1 teaspoon smoked paprika

½ teaspoon onion powder

½ teaspoon garlic powder

¼ teaspoon chili powder

¼ teaspoon kosher salt

4 slices sandwich bread

Vegan mayonnaise

Dijon mustard

6 thin tomato slices

Lettuce

BBQ Jackfruit Sandwich

In the last few years jackfruit, a cousin to figs and mulberries, has taken off in popularity, especially among vegans, who like its meatlike umami flavor and the fact that it has protein and other nutrients.

MAKES 4 LARGE OR
6 MEDIUM SANDWICHES

1-2 tablespoons (15-30 ml) cooking oil (any kind)

2 20-ounce (565 g) cans young green jackfruit in water

¼ cup (60 ml) Signature VBQ Spice Rub (see recipe, page 18)

1¼ cup (295 ml) Smoky Vidalia VBQ Sauce (see recipe, page 38)

4 to 6 whole-grain vegan buns

1 Rinse, drain, and thoroughly dry the jackfruit. Chop off the center "core" portion of the fruit and discard it. Place the jackfruit in a mixing bowl and prepare your smoker for a smoke at 165°–220°F (75°–105°C) for 15 minutes.

2 Remove the jackfruit from the smoker. Toss the jackfruit in the spice rub to coat.

3 Heat a large skillet over medium heat. Once hot, add the cooking oil and the seasoned jackfruit. Toss the jackfruit in the cooking oil to coat and cook for 2 to 3 minutes to achieve some color. Add ¾ cup (175 ml) of the Creole VBQ Sauce and thin with water to make a thinner sauce. Stir and reduce heat to medium-low and cook, covered, for about 20 minutes so that the jackfruit takes on the flavor of the sauce. Stir the mixture occasionally as it cooks.

4 Increase the heat to medium-high and cook for 2 to 3 minutes more to get a little extra color and texture. Then remove from the heat. Place generous portions of jackfruit on the bottom buns, top with the remaining Creole VBQ Sauce. Serve. (It is a hot sauce; use less or none for diners who do not like hot things.) Leftover jackfruit keeps for up to 2 days in the refrigerator, but it is best when fresh.

Smoked Garlic Naan Bread

The Indian flatbread naan is surprisingly easy to make, tastes great straight from the skillet, and tastes especially good with smoked garlic.

1 Smoke the garlic in your smoker for over low heat for 20 minutes.

2 Combine the flours, sugar, salt, yeast, yogurt, olive oil, and water in the bowl of a stand mixer fitted with the paddle attachment. Mix until you have a well-blended dough. Mince the garlic fine and add it to the dough mixture.

3 Knead the dough with your mixer's dough hook for 10 minutes. Transfer to a large bowl coated with cooking spray. Cover the bowl with wet paper towels and allow to rise for 1 hour. Then divide the dough into about ten 3-inch (8-cm)-diameter balls. Allow to rest 15 minutes, then roll dough out to ¼-inch (0.625-cm)-thick rounds.

4 Heat a nonstick skillet coated with cooking spray over medium-high heat. Cook the bread 2 minutes on each side or until golden brown, making sure to coat the pan with additional cooking spray between breads. Serve with your favorite topping, such as hummus or salsa, or just straight up with some extra virgin olive oil drizzled on top.

MAKES ABOUT 10 FLATBREADS

3 garlic cloves

2½ cups (10 g) unbleached all-purpose flour

½ cup (65 g) whole wheat flour

2 teaspoons (5 g) sugar

1½ teaspoons salt

1 package active dry yeast

¼ cup (60 g) vegan yogurt

1 tablespoon (15 ml) extra-virgin olive oil

1 cup (235 ml) water

Smoked Chopped Chick'n Sammie

When I needed a chick'n option on the menu to add to the barbecue variety, I created this riff on an Olive Garden classic, now vegan and with some other changes as well. It is, to this date, my biggest-selling sandwich. The texture alone will have you going insane!

MAKE THE SMOKED CHOPPED CHICK'N:

1   Combine the beans and their liquid, water, olive oil, miso, salt, granulated onion, granulated garlic, and vegan soup base in a blender. Blend until smooth.

2   Put the vital wheat gluten in a large bowl. Pour the blended mixture into the bowl, stirring until a ball of dough forms.

TO KNEAD THE DOUGH WITH A FOOD PROCESSOR:

3   Separate the dough into three equal balls. Using a plastic (recommended) or metal S-blade attachment, pulse each ball of dough for about 2 minutes, until the gluten has formed.

SERVES 6

SMOKED CHOPPED CHICK'N

1 (15.5-ounces/440 g) can white beans plus aquafaba (bean liquid)

6 tablespoons (90 ml) water

1 tablespoon (15 ml) extra-virgin olive oil

2 tablespoons (30 g) white miso paste

1 teaspoon kosher salt

1 tablespoon (5 g) granulated onion

1 tablespoon (5 g) granulated garlic

1 teaspoon vegan Better Than Bouillon No Chicken soup base (or substitute 1 bouillon cube)

2 cups (240 g) vital wheat gluten

SANDWICH FIXINGS

Sandwich fixings can be whatever you choose!

TO KNEAD THE DOUGH BY HAND:

4   Knead for 10 to 15 minutes, or until the dough is firm and elastic. Using your hands or a knife, separate the kneaded dough into three equal balls.

5   Wrap each of the three dough balls tightly in aluminum foil. Heat a few inches of water over high heat in a large pot or pan that will fit your steamer basket until it comes to a boil. Place the steamer basket in the pan, add the seitan to the basket, and cover the pan with a lid. Reduce the heat to medium-low and steam for 45 minutes. Flip the seitan, then steam again for another 45 minutes. Check in every so often to make sure that you pan has not run dry; add more water to the pan as needed.

6   Let the seitan cool in the aluminum foil for at least 10 minutes before unwrapping. When the seitan is cool enough to handle, begin shredding it with your hands. Pull apart the "chicken" shreds as thin or thick as you like.

7   Take your shredded chick'n and prep the smoker for 45-minute smoke session (165°–220°F [75°–105°C]). Remove your chick'n from the smoker. It is ready to be assembled.

8   Sandwich can be assembled any way you see fit, with all your desired fixings!

Smoked Reuben Sandwich

*There is absolutely nothing like a good deli sandwich.
There's something about the extra thin slices of the filling
with a crazy crusty bread! Yum! This Corned Veef recipe
will have your sandwiches standing up against the best in
New York. Forgetaboutit!*

1   Preheat the oven to 375°F (190°C).

MAKE THE CORNED VEEF:

2   Wrap the tofu in paper towels and squeeze out the extra
moisture with your hands. Break the tofu into chunks and add
it to a food processor. Add the apple juice, dill pickle juice, oil,
mustard, coconut aminos, bouillon cube, nutritional yeast,
chili powder, granulated garlic, granulated onion, coriander,
allspice, salt, pepper, and food coloring. Process until smooth
like a puree.

3   Add vital wheat gluten evenly over the top. Mix until just
combined; it's okay if you see a bit of flour on top.

4   Turn the dough onto a counter and knead 20 to 25 times, until
firm and elastic. Form the dough into a loaf shape. Set aside
while you make the brine.

Note   The casserole dish you use to bake the seitan must be
large enough to allow the seitan dough to double in size.

SERVES 2

CORNED VEEF SEITAN

1 (14-ounce/400 g) tub extra-firm tofu, drained

½ cup (120 ml) unsweetened apple juice

¼ cup (60 ml) dill pickle juice

2 tablespoons (30 ml) vegetable oil

1 tablespoon (10 g) Dijon mustard

1 tablespoon (15 ml) coconut aminos (or substitute soy sauce or Braggs)

1 not-beef bouillon cube

3 tablespoons (15 g) nutritional yeast

2 teaspoons chili powder

1 teaspoon granulated garlic

1 teaspoon granulated onion

½ teaspoon ground coriander

¼ teaspoon ground allspice

½ teaspoon kosher salt

¼ teaspoon freshly ground black pepper

About 10 drops red food coloring

1½ cups (180 g) vital wheat gluten

MAKE THE BRINE:

5 Combine the boiling water, soup base, pickling spice, white vinegar, and mustard in a large, deep casserole dish. Add the seitan loaf and cover tightly with aluminum foil.

6 Bake for 1½ hours, carefully flipping the seitan halfway through.

MAKE THE SPICE RUB:

7 While corned veef is cooking, mix together the mustard, oil, chili powder, coriander, and salt in a small bowl. Set aside.

8 Place the corned veef brisket on cutting board. Strain and reserve the brine. Wipe out the casserole dish. When cool enough to handle (after 10 to 15 minutes or so), rub the spice mix over the top and sides of corned veef and place it back in the same dish. Cover tightly with aluminum foil and bake for another 30 minutes.

9 When the brisket is done, let rest for 10 to 15 minutes to firm up. Take your brisket and prep your smoker for for a 60- to 90-minute-long smoke session over low heat.

10 Remove your brisket from the smoker and thinly slice.

11 To assemble the sandwiches, spread mustard on one side of the four slices of bread. Cover two slices with the sliced corned veef and sauerkraut. Top with the remaining bread, cut in halves, and serve.

BRINE

3 cups (705 ml) water, boiling

1 tablespoon (15 g) Better Than Bouillon No Beef soup base

2 tablespoons (55 g) mixed pickling spice

1 tablespoon (15 ml) distilled white vinegar

1 tablespoon (10 g) Dijon mustard

SPICE RUB

1 tablespoon (10 g) Dijon mustard

1 tablespoon (15 ml) vegetable oil

1½ teaspoons chili powder

1½ teaspoons ground coriander

¼ teaspoon kosher salt

SANDWICH FIXINGS

4 slices rye bread

Whole-grain mustard

½ cup (70 g) sauerkraut, well drained

Smoked Oyster Mushroom Banh Mi Sandwich

This is a sandwich I placed on the menu at my restaurant one summer, and it took off! Most of my specials consist of my favorite dishes, and Vietnamese banh mi are a weakness of mine. Combined with the spin of smoke, this kicked up version is a favorite.

1 Set your smoker to smoke for for 45 minutes over low heat.

MAKE THE PICKLE:

2 Combine the carrot, cucumber, sugar, salt, water, and rice wine vinegar.

3 Mix well to combine, then set aside and leave to pickle for at least 45 minutes, up to overnight.

MAKE THE MUSHROOMS:

4 Arrange the mushrooms in a single layer on a baking sheet. Season with salt and pepper and drizzle with a splash of olive oil. Add the garlic, hoisin sauce, and soy sauce and use a spoon to combine all the ingredients until the mushrooms are well coated.

5 Smoke the mushrooms for 45 minutes, or until cooked through and most of the moisture has evaporated. Remove the mushrooms from the smoker and shred the mushrooms with two forks.

SERVES 2

PICKLE

1 small carrot, cut into matchsticks

1 small cucumber, cut into matchsticks

2 tablespoons (30 g) sugar

1½ teaspoons kosher salt

¼ cup (60 ml) water

2 tablespoons (30 ml) rice wine vinegar

MUSHROOMS

1 pound (455 g) fresh shiitake mushrooms, stems discarded

Kosher salt and freshly ground black pepper

Extra-virgin olive oil

4 cloves garlic, thinly sliced

3 tablespoons (45 ml) hoisin sauce

2 tablespoons (30 ml) soy sauce

continued

MEANWHILE, MAKE THE SRIRACHA MAYO:

6 Combine the vegan mayo and sriracha sauce together in a small bowl.

TO SERVE:

7 Cut the baguette into quarters and slice each quarter open. Build the banh mi by spreading a heaped tablespoon of the sriracha mayo on the inside of each baguette. Drain the pickle, then add a handful of the pickled veg to each, followed by a generous helping of pulled mushrooms, some radishes, a small handful of cilantro leaves, and some chile slices. Finish with a squeeze of lime juice. Delicious!

SRIRACHA MAYO

6 tablespoons (80 g) vegan mayonnaise

2 tablespoons (30 ml) sriracha sauce

TO SERVE

1 baguette

4 radishes, thinly sliced

Large handful of fresh cilantro leaves picked off the stems

1 fresh red chile pepper, such as serrano, seeded (optional) and thinly sliced

1 lime

Veef Brisket Sandwich

Another OG classic. The very first recipe I ever attempted when coming over to the "bark" side… tree bark … vegan… nevermind. Just know it's crazy good.

1   Prepare your smoker for a solid 2 hours of smoke time, 165°–220°F (75°–105°C). Prepare a 9 × 13-inch (23 × 33 cm) baking dish by coating lightly with oil. Set aside. Preheat the oven to 375°F (190°C).

MAKE THE WET MIXTURE:

2   Combine the wine, tamari, maple syrup, hot sauce, vegetable stock, tomato paste, and oil in a large bowl and mix well.

MAKE THE DRY MIXTURE:

3   In a separate bowl, combine the wheat gluten, chickpea flour, chili powder, paprika, cumin, granulated onion, garlic granules, and salt. Mix well.

4   Combine the dry mixture with *half* of the wet mixture. Mix until combined completely. Knead for 3 minutes until all is mixed thoroughly and the dough if firm and elastic. Form into a brisket shape (a rectangle) and place in the prepared baking dish. Lightly coat the raw seitan with oil. Add the remaining wet mixture, pouring it around the baking dish and over the raw seitan.

5   Bake for 25 minutes. Flip the loaf over. Bake for another 20 minutes. A few minutes before it's done, remove the seitan and baste it with some of the remaining liquid in the dish. Return to the oven for another 5 to 10 minutes. The liquid should be almost evaporated and thickened.

SERVES 4

WET MIXTURE

1 cup (235 ml) Marsala wine

¼ cup (60 ml) tamari

¼ cup (85 g) pure maple syrup

2 tablespoons (30 ml) hot sauce

3½ cups (840 ml) vegetable stock

1 (8-ounce/225 g) can tomato paste

3 tablespoons (45 ml) vegetable oil

DRY MIXTURE

2¼ cups (270 g) vital wheat gluten

¾ cup (70 g) chickpea flour

2 tablespoons (15 g) chili powder

1 tablespoon (5 g) smoked paprika

1½ teaspoons ground cumin

2 tablespoons (20 g) granulated onion

2 tablespoons (20 g) granulated garlic

continued

6 Remove the brisket from the oven and leave to cool for a few minutes. Cover the seitan with the barbecue sauce, being sure it coats all sides well. Place in the smoker and smoke for 1 hour on each side over low heat.

7 Remove from the smoker. Slice the brisket as thin as you can and serve with all your desired fixins!

Vegetable oil

1 tablespoon (10 g) kosher salt

2 cups (475 ml) Smoky Vidalia VBQ Sauce (see recipe, page 38)

SANDWICH FIXINGS

Sandwich fixings can be whatever you choose!

Smoked TVP Patty Melt

There's something synonymous about big-ass sandwiches and barbecue. This patty melt version is a two-hander for sure.

MAKE THE ONIONS:

1   Heat the vegetable oil in a medium sauté pan over medium-low heat. Add the onions, sugar, and cider vinegar. Cook the onions for 30 minutes, stirring every few minutes, until the onions are dark and beginning to get jammy. Set the onions aside.

MAKE THE SPECIAL SAUCE:

2   Combine the mayonnaise, ketchup, relish, Worcestershire, and cayenne in a small bowl and mix well. Cover and refrigerate until you are ready to serve.

MAKE THE PATTIES:

3   Preheat a grill to medium heat, if using. Cook the burgers on the grill or in a sauté pan over medium heat for 3 minutes on each side, until the internal temperature reaches 165°F (74°C).

4   Keep the grill heated or heat a sauté pan over medium heat. Assemble the patty melts: Spread the melted butter on one side of each of the bread slices. Place two slices of American cheese each on the non-buttered sides of two slices of the bread, then add a burger on top of each. Spread the special sauce on top of the burgers, followed by half the onions and two slices of Swiss cheese. Top the burgers with the remaining slices of bread, buttered sides up.

5   Slide the assembled patty melts onto the grill or into a pan and use a flat pan lid or spatula to press them down. Cook for 1 minute, then carefully flip onto the other side, pressing down again. Remove from the grill after 1 minute, cut in half and serve immediately.

SERVES 2

ONIONS

1 tablespoon (15 ml) vegetable oil

2 cups (120 g) thinly sliced yellow onion

1 teaspoon sugar

1 teaspoon apple cider vinegar

SPECIAL SAUCE

¼ cup (60 g) vegan mayonnaise

1 tablespoon (15 g) ketchup

1 tablespoon (15 g) sweet pickle relish

⅛ teaspoon vegan Worcestershire sauce

Pinch of cayenne

PATTY MELT

2 TVP burger patties

2 tablespoons (30 g) unsalted vegan butter, melted

4 slices sourdough bread

4 slices vegan American cheese

4 slices vegan Swiss cheese

4

"Meaty"
Mains

Smoked Carrot Dawgz

Carrot… dawgz?? YES, carrot dawgs. This is always my sleeper go-to when I need to bring a dish to a cookout. Carrots and other root vegetables are dense and hearty enough to work as meat substitutes. With just the right amount of smoked flavor, these root vegetables can be the best guilt-free stadium food you ever had. Pair these bad boys with some nice hearty potato salad.

1 Use a peeler to shape the carrots into hot dog shapes and cut to the length of the buns.

2 Bring a medium pot of salted water to a boil, add the carrots, and boil until fork tender, about 10 minutes. Drain the carrots and rinse with cold water until cooled. Place in a zippered bag.

3 Whisk together the soy sauce, cider vinegar, maple syrup, liquid smoke, mustard, garlic, granulated onion, and salt and pour into the bag with the carrots. Marinate for at least 4 hours; overnight is better. The longer they marinate, the more dawg flavor.

4 Remove the carrots from the bag and pat dry. Prepare the dawgz at 85°–120°F (30°–50°C) for 20 minutes.

5 To serve, heat the oil in a skillet over medium heat. Sear the dawgz until browned all over. Slip into buns and top your dawgz with all of your favorite toppings.

SERVES 6 TO 8

DAWGZ

6 to 8 carrots, peeled

¼ cup (60 ml) soy sauce

¼ cup (60 ml) apple cider vinegar

2 tablespoons (30 ml) pure maple syrup

1 tablespoon (15 ml) liquid smoke

1 teaspoon yellow mustard

1 teaspoon minced garlic

1 teaspoon granulated onion

1 teaspoon kosher salt

TO SERVE

1 tablespoon (15 ml) vegetable oil

6 to 8 hot dog buns

Toppings, such as slaw and vegan Cincinnati chili

Smoked VBQ Meatless Loaf

The meatloaf was modernized in the 1960s and appeared on everyone's dinner table growing up. By far one of my favorite classic dishes, I had to create my own meatless version. Here textured vegetable protein, or TVP, a plant-based ingredient made of soy protein, gives the dish its meaty texture. Pair this recipe with my Loaded Mash Potato Casserole (see recipe, page 154) and VBQ Green Beans (see recipe, page 136).

1   Preheat the oven to 375°F (190°C). Line a 9 × 5-inch (23 × 13-cm) loaf pan with parchment paper.

2   Combine the TVP, vegetable broth, and soy sauce in a medium bowl and mix until combined. Let sit for about 10 minutes, until the liquid is absorbed. Add the oats, flax meal, nutritional yeast, onion, garlic, celery, granulated onion, granulated garlic, oregano, and basil. Pack into the prepared loaf pan.

3   Bake for 40 to 45 minutes, until the texture is firm and dense. Remove from the oven, remove the loaf from the pan, and let cool for 10 to 20 minutes. Take the loaf and smoke at 165°–220°F (75°–105°C) for 30 to 45 minutes.

4   To serve, pour the barbecue sauce over the loaf, slice, and serve.

SERVES 4

2 cups (200 g) TVP (textured vegetable protein)

2 cups (475 ml) vegetable broth

2 tablespoons (30 ml) soy sauce

1 cup (80 g) quick oats

¼ cup (25 g) ground flax meal

2 tablespoons (10 g) nutritional yeast

½ cup (40 g) minced onion

¼ cup (60 g) minced garlic

¼ cup (25 g) chopped celery

1 teaspoon granulated onion

1 teaspoon granulated garlic

1 teaspoon dried oregano

1 teaspoon dried basil

1 cup (235 ml) Smoky Vidalia VBQ Sauce (see recipe, page 38)

Smoky Rack of Riibz

You can't have good "que" without tender smoky ribs (animal free, of course)! This recipe will provide you that smoky, tender, savory, sweet barbecue taste that will have your biggest carnivorous friend contemplating life! You will need 6 to 8 bamboo skewers (¼-inch/5-mm) thick. These will be your "bones." Pair with our Smoked Mac 'n' Cheeze (see recipe, page 168) and Smoky Collard Greens (see recipe, page 132).

1   Preheat the oven to 425°F (220°C).

2   Shred or chop the jackfruit. You can use a knife or pulse with a food processor for this.

3   Combine the wheat gluten, soy protein, chickpea flour, flax meal, nutritional yeast, onion powder, granulated garlic, paprika, cumin, and cayenne in a large bowl and mix until incorporated. Add the shredded jackfruit, oil, and 1 cup (235 ml) of the vegetable stock and mix until blended. The consistency should resemble bread dough.

4   Transfer the mixture to a work surface and use a rolling pin to roll flat into a ½-inch (1 cm) sheet. Stick the bamboo skewers into the side of your sheet about an inch (2.5 cm) apart from each other. This is your riib rack.

continued

SERVES 4

20-ounce (565 g) can young jackfruit, drained and rinsed

1¼ cups (190 g) vital wheat gluten

2 tablespoons (12 g) soy protein

1 tablespoon (5 g) chickpea flour

1 tablespoon (5 g) flax meal

2 tablespoons (10 g) nutritional yeast

1 teaspoon granulated onion

1 teaspoon granulated garlic

1 tablespoon (5 g) smoked paprika

1 teaspoon ground cumin

½ teaspoon cayenne pepper

8 cups (2 L) vegetable stock

2 tablespoons (30 ml) oil (any oil will do)

½ cup (85 g) Signature VBQ Spice Rub (see recipe, page 18)

1 cup (235 ml) Smoky Vidalia VBQ Sauce (see recipe, page 38) (optional)

5   Place the riib rack into a 9 × 13-inch (23 × 33-cm) baking pan and cover with remaining 7 cups (1.6 L) vegetable stock. Cover the baking dish with aluminum foil. Place on the bottom rack of your oven and bake for 60 minutes. Remove the riib rack from the pan and rub both sides generously with the spice rub. Return to the oven to bake for another 30 minutes.

6   Now it is time to smoke! Smoke at 165°–220°F (75°–105°C) for 30 to 45 minutes.

7   Remove the riib rack from the smoker and cut rib in between each skewer to create individual "ribs." Brush on the barbecue sauce or serve as is.

Note   You can substitute pea protein for the soy protein if you're looking to go soy free. You can find it in the baking aisle of your local grocery store.

Smoky Bacun Potato Skinnies

Despite the name, these will not make you skinny! But they will remind you of a tailgate filled with great food and excitement. Topped with smoky bacun, this classic will keep your spirits up. While the potatoes bake, make the toppings.

1 Preheat the oven to 400°F (200°C). Line a baking sheet with aluminum foil.

BAKE THE POTATOES:

2 Rub the potatoes lightly with vegetable oil and bake them on the prepared baking sheet until their skins are crisp and a fork easily slides into their flesh, about 30 minutes. Transfer the potatoes to a wire rack and let cool for 10 minutes.

3 When the potatoes are cool enough to touch, cut each in half and gently scoop the flesh from the skin, leaving about ¼-inch (5 mm) or more of the flesh. Reserve the scooped potatoes for potato soup or crispy potato pancakes. Bake the hollowed skins another 15 minutes.

4 Remove from oven and top each skin with cheese, using 2 to 4 teaspoons (5 to 10 g) for each skin. Bake an additional 15 minutes and broil for another 5 minutes, or until the cheese begins to bubble. Remove from the heat and transfer to a serving dish. Season with salt and pepper.

TO MAKE THE DIP:

5 Combine the vegan sour cream, vegan mayonnaise, almond milk, chives, granulated garlic, and dill. Season to taste with salt and pepper. Cover and refrigerate until you are ready to serve.

SERVES 6

POTATOES

1- to 2-pound (.5 to 1 kg) bag yellow-flesh potatoes (I use small potatoes)

Vegetable oil, for brushing potatoes

1 cup (120 g) vegan cheese shreds (Daiya Cheddar is recommended)

Kosher salt and freshly ground black pepper

SOUR CREAM DIP

½ cup (115 g) vegan sour cream

¼ cup (55 g) vegan mayonnaise

¼ cup (60 ml) unsweetened almond milk

1 tablespoon (5 g) minced fresh chives

½ teaspoon granulated garlic

⅛ teaspoon dried dill

Kosher salt and freshly ground black pepper

continued

89

TO MAKE THE TVP BACON BITS:

6   Combine the water and bouillon in a medium saucepan and bring to a boil over high heat. Once water reaches a hard, rolling boil, remove from heat and add the TVP and Worcestershire, mixing to combine. You'll notice the TVP absorbs water and this is good because we want to rehydrate it. Set aside and let it rehydrate for 15 to 20 minutes, until all the water is absorbed.

7   Heat the oil in a small skillet over medium-low heat. Add the rehydrated TVP and pan-fry until it turns dark brown and crispy, resembling real bacon bits, 15 to 20 minutes, stirring the mixture every 3 to 5 minutes or so.

8   Once the TVP bacon bits reach a color and consistency of your liking, transfer to a paper towel–lined plate and set aside.

9   To serve, garnish the potatoes with the chives and bacon bits and serve the sour cream dip on the side.

TVP BACON BITS

½ cup (120 ml) boiling water

1 teaspoon Better Than Bouillon Vegetarian No Chicken soup base

½ cup (65 g) TVP (textured vegetable protein)

1 teaspoon vegan Worcestershire sauce

3 tablespoons (45 ml) vegetable oil, for pan frying

Chopped chives, for garnishing

Kosher salt (optional)

Smoked Sweet Potato Burnt Ends

Here in the South, burnt ends aren't really a staple in our pits. That honor belongs to Kansas City! Putting a little twist on ours, we're using the mighty sweet potato. It gives us that dense meaty texture were looking for when it comes to burnt ends. Plus the bonus sweetness it adds complements any kind of barbecue rub or sauce. Pair with our Smoked Stout Beer Baked Beans (see recipe, page 126).

1 Combine the sweet potatoes with 4 quarts (4 L) water in a large stockpot. Add the thyme, garlic, salt, lemon juice, and liquid smoke. Bring the water to a boil, then reduce to a simmer. Cook until fork tender, about 30 minutes.

2 Remove the potatoes from heat and drain. Discard the thyme and garlic. Allow the potatoes to cool to the touch.

3 Toss the potatoes gently with oil in a large bowl; try not to break potatoes during tossing. Liberally sprinkle the spice rub over the potatoes. Be sure to coat as evenly as possible.

4 Arrange the potatoes on aluminum foil–lined smoker and smoke at 85°–120°F (30°–50°C) for 20 minutes.

5 Remove the potatoes from smoker and arrange on a serving dish. Pour the sauce over the potatoes or serve on the side for dipping, garnish with the scallions, and serve.

SERVES 4

2 pounds (1 kg) sweet potatoes cut into ¼-inch (5-mm) pieces

1 sprig fresh thyme

3 cloves garlic

1 tablespoon (10 g) kosher salt

2 tablespoons (30 ml) fresh lemon juice

1 tablespoon (15 ml) liquid smoke

3 tablespoons (45 ml) vegetable oil

¾ cup (125 g) Signature VBQ Spice Rub (see recipe, page 18)

1 cup (235 ml) Smoky Vidalia VBQ Sauce (see recipe, page 38)

¼ cup (25 g) sliced scallions, green and white parts

Smoked Carrot Lox & Bagels

The idea behind this recipe started in my NYC travels. I often struggle with finding quality vegan breakfast options outside of smoothies. I'm a savory guy! So I stumbled into this corner deli that advertised vegan lox. So I drilled him about the main ingredients and said once I touched down home, this is getting freaked!

SERVES 4 TO 6

2 cups (600 g) kosher salt, plus more if needed

3 large carrots (do not peel)

1 tablespoon (15 ml) extra-virgin olive oil, plus more as needed

2 teaspoons liquid smoke

½ teaspoon coconut vinegar

Toasted bagels, capers, vegan cream cheese, red onion, and dill sprigs, to serve

1   Preheat the oven to 375°F (190°C).

2   To slow roast the carrots, spread 1 cup (300 g) of the salt in a glass pyrex baking dish that offers just enough room to accommodate the length and width of the carrots so you can keep them whole. Rinse the unpeeled carrots and place them wet into the salt, making sure that the carrots are nestled in the salt and do not make contact with the bottom of the pan. Pour the remaining whole cup (300 g) of salt evenly over the tops, adding a bit more as needed to ensure they are fully covered in salt.

3   Roast, uncovered, for 1½ hours.

4   Tip the baking dish onto a baking sheet and allow the carrots to cool just enough so you can handle them. Crack away and brush off any salt, then peel away the skin. It's fine if there is still some skin left on the carrot. Then, using a mandolin or sharp knife, thinly slice the carrots into jagged, thin strips. Place into a clean glass container.

5   To marinate the carrots, whisk together the olive oil, liquid smoke, and coconut vinegar. (If you have a little more or little less than 1½ cups [355 ml] carrot, just add a little more or less of the liquid components as needed.) Drizzle the marinade over the warm carrots and toss well to coat. At this point, the flavor will not taste very "lox like"—they will need to be placed in the refrigerator for at least two days to allow the flavor to deepen and mellow, and for the carrots to get really soft and silky. If the carrots start to look dry during marinating time, add an additional tablespoon (15 ml) of olive oil and give it a good stir. (You want the carrots to look soft and slightly shiny throughout the marinating time.)

6   To serve, remove the carrots from the refrigerator and allow to come to room temperature. Then serve with toasted bagels, capers, vegan cream cheese, red onion, and dill as desired.

Smoked Vegan Wings

More than a few of my customers—and my friends—say they like these better than the so-called "real thing." For me, these are the quintessential party food.

1 Make a spice mix: In a medium bowl, mix together the onion powder and the garlic powder with the smoked paprika, cayenne, cumin, oregano, salt, and pepper. Meanwhile, preheat your oven to 300°F (149°C) and prepare your smoker for a low-heat smoke.

2 Add the "wings" to the bowl, cover the bowl with a plate, and shake well to coat the "wings" well and evenly with the spices. Spread the "wings" in one layer on a non-stick or silicone baking sheet, or on a regular baking sheet lined with parchment paper. Drizzle the "wings" on both sides lightly with the maple syrup.

3 Bake the "wings" in the oven for about 10 minutes, turning them over halfway through, until the spice coating is just beginning to get crispy and just starts to brown.

4 Transfer the "wings" to the smoker and smoke for 20 minutes in low heat, or until the outer surface of the "wings" is a beautiful dark red color.

5 Serve with hot sauce, as I do, or, if you like, with vegan ranch dressing.

SERVES 2 TO 4

¾ teaspoon garlic powder

¾ teaspoon onion powder

½ teaspoon sweet smoked paprika

¼ teaspoon cayenne pepper

¼ teaspoon ground cumin

¼ teaspoon dried oregano

½ teaspoon kosher salt

¼ teaspoon black pepper

10 seitan "chicken" wings (available in the vegan frozen foods section of many supermarkets, or in Asian markets)

2 teaspoons (15 g) maple syrup

½ cup (110 g) bottled hot sauce, such as Frank's Red Hot

Smoked Veef Lasagna

My childhood wrapped into one pan! Lasagna is the best thing to make for a family. This version has a bit of a smoky flavor that pairs well with the vine-ripened tomatoes. There will be no need to boil your pasta noodles. Your sauce will cook the dry pasta just fine.

1   Preheat the oven to 350°F (180°C).

2   Heat the olive oil in a pan over medium heat. Add the onion, garlic, and Italian seasoning and sauté for about 5 minutes, until the onions are translucent and fragrant. Add the tomato puree, salt, and pepper. Cook for another 10 minutes over low heat. Add the vegan beef and stir to combine. Cook for about 3 minutes. Taste and adjust the seasoning accordingly. Reduce the heat to medium low, add the tomato puree and stir to combine, for about 3 minutes. Taste and add salt accordingly. Remove from heat and set aside.

3   Set aside 1 cup (115 g) of the vegan mozzarella cheese (this will be for the top layer). In a 9 × 13-inch (23 × 33-cm) pan, spread ½ cup (120 g) of the "meat" marinara sauce mixture evenly on the bottom. Cover with about 4 lasagna noodles lengthwise, overlapping a bit. This will be your first layer.

4   Next, add about 1 cup (240 g) of the "meat" marinara sauce mixture (just ensure you have enough for four even layers) and then one-third of the vegan ricotta, and about one-third of the remaining vegan mozzarella on top of the ricotta.

5   Repeat the layers until you've reached the top layer. Add the remaining "meat" sauce on top, then sprinkle over the reserved 1 cup vegan mozzarella.

6   Cover the pan with foil and bake for 30 minutes.

7   Remove the pan from the oven and take it straight to the smoker for a 1-hour smoke session over low heat. The smoke will be absorbed mostly into your cheeze topping, but that's the fun part!

8   Put the lasagna under the broiler and broil for 3 to 5 minutes on low to brown the cheese on top. Top with basil, and allow to set up on the counter for about 10 minutes before cutting into slices. Cut into nine to twelve even slices. Serve and enjoy.

SERVES 6

1½ tablespoons (25 ml) extra-virgin olive oil

1 medium white onion, diced

5 cloves, garlic minced

2 tablespoons (30 g) Italian seasoning

1½ (30-ounce/795 g) cans tomato puree

¾ teaspoon kosher salt

½ teaspoon freshly ground black pepper

9 to 12 ounces (255 to 340 g) Smoked Veef Brisket (see recipe, page 75) or vegan meat alternative crumbles

3 cups (345 g) shredded vegan mozzarella

2 cups (475 ml) vegan ricotta

16 lasagna noodles

Basil, for garnish

Smoked Shredded Mushroom Carnitas

Tacos have quickly become an American staple, and carnitas is a popular filling. When there's tacos involved, you know there's a party! Our version is centered around the summer barbecue. These killer carnitas are simple yet crazy good. Serve in tortillas with your favorite toppings. I like to keep it simple with cilantro, onion, and our Smoked Pineapple Salsa (see recipe, page 41).

1   Prepare your smoker for a 40-minute smoke session over low heat. Line a baking sheet with parchment paper.

2   Trim the ends of the king trumpet mushrooms, shred the stems and caps between two forks, and put in a small bowl. Add the oregano, cumin, coriander, ¼ teaspoon of the salt, black pepper to taste, and 1 tablespoon (15 ml) of the olive oil. Toss well to coat. Spread evenly over the lined baking sheet.

3   Smoke for 40 minutes, until the mushrooms are chewy with some crispy ends, stirring halfway through for even cooking.

4   Heat a large skillet over medium-low heat and add the remaining 1 tablespoon (15 ml) of the oil along with the onion, garlic, jalapeño, and a pinch of salt. Sauté until soft, translucent, and lightly caramelized, 8 to 10 minutes.

5   Add the smoked mushrooms, orange juice, and vegan Worcestershire sauce, if using, and salt and pepper to taste. Sauté until the juice is absorbed and the mushrooms are sticky, stirring just once or twice to allow the mushrooms to crisp on a couple of sides, about 5 minutes. Serve warm.

SERVES 6

10 ounces (280 g) king trumpet mushrooms (5 to 6 large mushrooms)

2 teaspoons dried oregano

1½ teaspoons ground cumin

1 teaspoon ground coriander

Kosher salt and freshly ground black pepper

2 tablespoons (30 ml) extra-virgin olive oil

1 small white onion, finely diced

4 cloves garlic, minced

1 jalapeño, seeded (for less heat) and diced

½ cup (120 ml) fresh orange juice (1 to 2 oranges)

1 teaspoon vegan Worcestershire sauce (optional)

Smoked "Pigs" in a Blanket

Kids love these little carrot piggies in a blanket. Carrots hold flavors extremely well and when cooked can take on the texture of meat.

1   Pick through the baby carrots and set aside any weirdly shaped or super skinny ones (save for another use). If you want to use all of the crescent roll dough, choose 32 carrots to use.

2   Bring a medium pot of salted water to a boil. Add the baby carrots and boil until just tender, 10 to 12 minutes. You don't want them so soft that they're going to fall apart, but you won't want them to be super crunchy either. Check them frequently. When they get to the perfect texture, drain.

3   Transfer the boiled carrots to a shallow dish or a quart-size, zippered bag. Add the soy sauce, vegetable stock, cider vinegar, liquid smoke, maple syrup, granulated garlic, coconut aminos, black pepper, granulated onion, and paprika. Cover the dish or seal the bag and give the carrots a good shake.

4   Marinate for at least 4 hours in the fridge. Overnight is ideal. Give them a shake every hour or so when you think about it.

5   Roll out the crescent roll triangles and cut into halves.

6   Drain and rinse the marinated carrots.

7   Preheat the oven to 375°F (190°C). Line two baking sheets with parchment paper. Roll the carrots up in the dough and place on the prepared baking sheet about 2 inches apart. Bake for 12 to 14 minutes, until golden brown. Serve hot.

SERVES 6

1 (16-ounce/455 g) bag baby carrots

⅓ cup (80 ml) soy sauce

⅓ cup (80 ml) vegetable stock

1 tablespoon (15 ml) apple cider vinegar

1 teaspoon liquid smoke

1 teaspoon pure maple syrup

1 teaspoon granulated garlic

½ teaspoon coconut aminos

½ teaspoon freshly ground black pepper

½ teaspoon granulated onion

¼ teaspoon smoked paprika

2 (8-ounce/225 g) cans crescent rolls

Slow Cooker VBQ Chili

I've had the pleasure of participating in a few chili cookoffs, and this vegan version has stood up to the best of the best. This is a great dish for camping and other outdoor events.

1   Combine the beans, tomatoes, diced veef, water, garlic, Mexican oregano, paprika, liquid smoke, cumin, chili powder, ancho chile powder, and granulated onion in a 2- to 2½-quart (2 to 2.5 L) slow cooker. Cook on low for 4 hours.

2   Stir in the nutritional yeast and add salt to taste. Adjust any other seasoning as needed. Serve hot.

SERVES 6

1 (14.5-ounce/410 g) can pinto beans, drained and rinsed

1 (14.5 ounce/410 g) can diced tomatoes with green chiles

1 cup (235 ml) diced Veef Brisket (see recipe, page 75) or other vegan crumble

¼ cup (60 ml) water

2 cloves garlic, minced

1 teaspoon dried Mexican oregano

1 teaspoon smoked paprika

Few drops liquid smoke

½ teaspoon ground cumin

½ teaspoon chili powder, or more to taste

½ teaspoon ancho chile powder

½ teaspoon granulated onion

2 tablespoons (10 g) nutritional yeast, or to taste

Kosher salt

Smoked Brunswick Stewie

Brunswick Stew is a restaurant's dream recipe. It takes all of the leftovers from the day and turns them into liquid gold. This barbecue classic is what I call an anytime meal!

1   Heat the oil in a large pot over medium heat, for about 1 minute. Add the onion and sauté for about 5 minutes, stirring frequently, until it begins to soften. Add the jackfruit and tempeh bacon and break up the pieces of jackfruit and tempeh with a spoon as they cook. You can also use a fork to pull apart chunks of jackfruit. Cook for about 5 minutes, until the tempeh begins to brown. Add the garlic and cook it for about a minute, until very fragrant. Stir in the broth, tomatoes, barbecue sauce, Worcestershire sauce, liquid smoke, cayenne pepper, and okra. Bring to a boil, lower the heat, and allow the stew to simmer, stirring occasionally, until it thickens and the okra becomes tender, about 30 minutes.

2   Stir in the corn and lima beans. Continue simmering the stew for a minute, just to heat the veggies.

3   Remove the pot from the heat and season the stew with salt, pepper, and hot sauce to taste.

SERVES 6

2 tablespoons extra-virgin olive oil

1 large onion, diced

20-ounce (565 g) can young jackfruit, drained and rinsed

2 strips tempeh bacon (Lightlife Organic Tempeh Strips Fakin Bacon is recommended), chopped

3 cloves garlic, minced

2 cups (475 ml) vegetable broth

1 (14.5 ounce/410 g) can diced tomatoes with its juice

¾ cup (175 ml) Smoky Vidalia VBQ Sauce (see recipe, page 38)

2 tablespoons (30 ml) vegan Worcestershire sauce

½ teaspoon liquid smoke, or more to taste

½ teaspoon cayenne pepper

2 cups (200 g) trimmed and chopped fresh okra (1-inch/2.5 cm) pieces

1 cup (135 g) frozen corn, thawed

1 cup (165 g) frozen lima beans, thawed

Kosher salt and freshly ground black pepper

Hot sauce

Smoked Jambalaya

My personal take on the Creole classic, but without shrimp, chicken, or other meats.

1   Heat the oil in a large saucepan over medium heat. Add the carrot, bell pepper, and leek. Cook for 5 minutes, until the pepper and leek are fairly soft and just beginning to brown (the carrot will still be a bit hard). Add the garlic and minced chili and cook for a couple more minutes. Add the rice, vegetable stock, kidney beans, tomato puree, paprika, turmeric, thyme, oregano, and black pepper. Mix well.

2   Bring to a gentle simmer; you may need to turn the heat down a little. Allow to cook gently until the rice is tender, 10 to 12 minutes. You'll need to stir fairly regularly to prevent the rice from sticking, especially toward the end. If the rice is still not quite cooked when all the liquid has been absorbed, add a dash more water. Add the tomato, cook for 2 more minutes to heat through, and serve topped with plenty of fresh parsley.

SERVES 4

1 tablespoon (15 ml) extra-virgin olive oil

1 large carrot, finely diced

1 green bell pepper, finely diced

1 small leek, finely diced

2 cloves garlic, minced

½ teaspoon chili pepper paste, any brand

1 cup (185 g) white rice

3 cups (710 ml) vegetable stock

¼ cup (325 g) canned, rinsed, and drained kidney beans

1 tablespoon (30 ml) tomato puree or paste

2 teaspoons smoked paprika

1 teaspoon ground turmeric

½ teaspoon dried thyme

½ teaspoon dried oregano

Freshly ground black pepper

1 large tomato, cut into wedges

Chopped fresh flat-leaf parsley, to garnish

Smoked Chick'n Alfredo

It's hard to find a good Alfredo in the vegan world. I tinkered with this recipe for a while, and the texture and flavor is pretty spot on.

1 Bring a large pot of salted water to a boil, add the pasta, and cook according to package instructions. Drain, then return it to the pot and cover until the sauce is done.

2 Bring 4 cups (1 L) of water to a boil. Pour the hot water over the cashews and let soak for 5 minutes.

3 Meanwhile, heat the olive oil in a small pan over medium heat. Add the onion and garlic and sauté for 5 minutes, until the garlic is fragrant and the onion is translucent. Remove from heat.

4 Drain the cashews and discard the soaking water. Transfer the cashews to a high-power blender along with the onions and garlic, Italian seasoning, oat milk, nutritional yeast, lemon juice, and salt. Blend until very smooth. Add the smoked shredded chicken.

5 Pour the sauce over the pasta and stir. If the noodles are still hot, you may not need to cook it any more. If you want, heat the pasta with the alfredo sauce on low heat until warm. If it becomes too thick, add a bit of water to thin out the sauce. Serve immediately.

SERVES 2

12 ounces fettuccine

1½ cups (180 g) raw cashews

2 tablespoons (30 ml) extra-virgin olive oil

½ medium sweet onion, chopped

6 cloves garlic, minced

1 teaspoon dried Italian seasoning

2 cups (475 ml) unsweetened oat milk

¼ cup (15 g) nutritional yeast

1 tablespoon (15 ml) fresh lemon juice

1 teaspoon kosher salt, or to taste

Smoked Chopped Chick'n (see recipe, page 68) or Caring brand smoked vegan chicken

Smoked Crabby Cakes

Trust me, if you have had "real" crab cakes you will be amazed at how close these vegan ones taste to the original.

1　Add the garbanzo beans and hearts of palm to the bowl of a food processor. Pulse just a few times to break everything up. The results should have a crab-like consistency. (You can also do this manually, just by using a fork to shred everything up.) Set aside.

2　In a large mixing bowl, whisk the reserved bean liquid well until it is foamy. Then add the vegan mayonnaise, lemon juice, liquid smoke, Worcestershire sauce, mustard, and all the dry seasonings. Whisk to combine well.

3　Now add the breadcrumbs and green onions and the hearts of palm and garbanzo bean mixture. Gently fold to combine. Taste for seasoning, and add more if needed. Place the mixture in the freezer for 20 minutes. This helps the mixture stay together.

4　Take the "crab" mixture out of freezer. Place about ¼ cup of mixture into your hands and form a ball, then gently flatten the ball it into a patty shape. Repeat with the remaining "crab" mixture. Place enough breadcrumbs onto a shallow plate to coat the "crab" patties evenly. Coat each patty in the breadcrumbs on each side. Set aside.

5　Heat a large skillet over medium heat for 2 to 3 minutes. Add about 2 tablespoons of oil and pan-fry about 4 to 5 patties at a time for 3 to 4 minutes on each side, or until golden brown. Try to flip each patty only once. When done, transfer the patties to a paper towel-lined plate to absorb excess oil. Wipe out pan and add fresh oil as each new batch of uncooked patties is added. Serve hot with vegan tartar sauce and a lemon wedge and top with chopped green onions. Enjoy!

MAKES 12 MEDIUM CRAB CAKES

1 (15-ounce [425 g]) can garbanzo beans, rinsed and drained but with ¼ cup of the liquid reserved

2 (14-ounce [425 ml]) cans of hearts of palm, rinsed, drained, and cut in half lengthwise

¼ cup (60 g) vegan mayonnaise

1 teaspoon vegan Worcestershire sauce

1 teaspoon liquid smoke

1 teaspoon fresh lemon juice, or more to taste

1 teaspoon dijon mustard

½ cup (80 g) sliced green onion

2 teaspoons (5 g) kelp granules (can be found at Asian markets) or crushed dried seaweed

1 tablespoon (10 g) dried parsley

1½ teaspoons Old Bay Seasoning or other Creole- or Southern-style seafood seasoning

½ teaspoon sea salt, or more to taste

1 teaspoon granulated garlic

1 cup breadcrumbs (60 g) (panko or regular), plus more for breaded coating

¼ cup oil (60 ml) for pan-frying

Vegan tartar sauce, to serve

Lemon wedge(s), to serve

Chopped green onions, to serve

Smoked Teriyaki "Salmon" Fillet

Vegan Salmon? How? Well, it's all about texture and the re-creation of flavor. It's amazing the flaky ocean taste you get from this recipe.

1   Prepare the tofu by draining it, wrapping in paper towels, and pressing it for 15 to 30 minutes, until firm. Cut the tofu in half lengthwise, then in half lengthwise again, making four long, skinny strips of tofu. Take one piece of tofu and place a chopstick on either side of the tofu to stop you from cutting all the way through, so the slices remain intact. Slice the tofu partway through repeatedly about ⅛-inch (5 mm) apart to give the tofu a flaky texture. Repeat with the other tofu slices. Be careful handling them as they will be fragile.

2   Tear 1 sheet of nori into pieces. Combine the torn nori in a blender with the vegetable broth, cider vinegar, beet juice, miso, granulated garlic, salt, and turmeric. Blend until as smooth as possible. Place the tofu in a zippered bag or dish and cover it with the marinade. Let marinate for a minimum of 30 minutes, or overnight in the fridge.

3   Put the cornstarch into a wide bowl or baking dish. Cut the remaining nori into strips roughly the same size as the tofu pieces. Gently remove a tofu piece from the marinade (be careful as it will be fragile). Dunk a strip of the nori into the marinade, then stick it to the back of the tofu. (Covering the nori in the marinade will help it stick to the tofu). Dredge the tofu with the nori attached in the cornstarch, covering all sides of the tofu. Repeat with all the tofu pieces.

SERVES 4

1 (12.3-ounce/350 g) block extra-firm tofu

2 sheets nori

1 cup (235 ml) vegetable broth

3 tablespoons (45 ml) apple cider vinegar

½ cup beet juice

2 tablespoons (30 g) white miso paste

1 teaspoon granulated garlic

1 teaspoon kosher salt

½ teaspoon ground turmeric

½ cup (65 g) cornstarch, plus more if needed

2 tablespoons light oil, for frying

½ cup (120 ml) teriyaki sauce or marinade

Lemon wedges, for garnish (optional)

continued

4   Heat the oil in a large skillet or frying pan over medium-high
    heat. When hot, add the cornstarch-covered tofu. Fry for 2 to
    4 minutes per side, until lightly golden all over. Transfer to a
    baking dish and arrange in a single layer. Baste the fried tofu
    with the teriyaki marinade.

5   Prepare your smoker for a 10-minute smoke session over
    low heat.

6   Smoke your salmon just enough to establish a bit of flavor,
    about 10 minutes. Remove from the smoker and serve. Garnish
    with lemon wedges.

Vegan Pasta Bolognese

The ubiquitous American dish known as "pasta with meat sauce" is known in Italy and the rest of Europe as "pasta Bolognese." Here is a terrific vegan spin on the classic dish.

1 Place a large saucepan over medium heat and add the olive oil. When hot, add the onion and saute for 2 minutes or until it just begins to turning soft. Add the carrot and celery then saute for 2 minutes more, then add the garlic and cook for another 2 minutes.

2 Stir in the vegan ground "meat" and saute, stirring occasionally, for 5 minutes. Stir in the tomato paste, soy sauce, vegan Worcestershire sauce, and chopped tomatoes. Fill the empty can of chopped tomatoes up with just boiled water and stir in the vegan beef powder. Add to the saucepan and stir to combine. Bring the sauce to a simmer, then stir in the bay leaf, salt, pepper, and sugar. Cover the saucepan with a lid and leave to simmer for 30 minutes, stirring occasionally.

3 While the sauce cooks, cook your pasta or other noodles according to the packet instructions or until al dente. Drain the pasta, but reserve about 1 cup (235 ml) of the pasta water. Check the sauce; it should be reduced and very thick. Add a dash of the pasta water to the sauce and stir to loosen things up. Finally stir through the liquid smoke.

4 Return the cooked pasta to its saucepan and dress with a little sauce. Divide the pasta among 4 plates and top with the remaining sauce. Serve with extra black pepper, a sprinkle of fresh parsley, or your favorite vegan Parmesan.

SERVES 4

2 tablespoons (30 ml) olive oil or vegetable oil

1 onion, peeled and finely diced

1 carrot, peeled and finely diced

1 celery stalk, finely diced

1 garlic clove, finely minced or crushed

3 cups (345 g) of your favorite vegan ground meat substitute

1 tablespoon (15 g) tomato paste

2 teaspoons (10 ml) dark soy sauce

16-ounce (455 g) can chopped tomatoes

1 teaspoon vegan Worcestershire sauce

2 teaspoons (10 ml) vegan beef stock powder

1 bay leaf

2 teaspoons (5 g) sea salt

½ teaspoon ground black pepper

1 teaspoon sugar

16 ounces (455 g) dry pasta or glass noodles

2 teaspoons (10 ml) liquid smoke

Fresh parsley, for garnish, optional

Vegan Parmesan, for garnish, optional

Smoked Beer and Fennel Bratwurst

Sound the alarms! Summer's in the air! Once the brats come out and hit the smoker, it's an official party! These vegan brats are drenched in IPA and spiced with fennel. Add some caramelized onion and serve in a pretzel bun. Game over!

1 Combine the wheat gluten, nutritional yeast, fennel seeds, granulated garlic, granulated onion, sage, mustard powder, smoked paprika, salt, black pepper, and allspice in a large bowl. Whisk together until thoroughly combined.

2 Combine the beans, miso, soy sauce, beer, and liquid smoke in a food processor and process until thoroughly mixed and smooth.

3 Add the wet ingredients to dry and mix to form a loose dough. Cover and let rest while cutting five large square sheets of aluminum foil and preparing the smoker for a 45-minute smoke session (165°–220°F [75°–105°C]).

4 Pour 1 to 2 inches (2.5 to 5 cm) of water into a baking pan.

5 Cut the dough into five equal pieces and shape into logs 5 to 6 inches (13 to 15 cm) long.

6 Roll each log in foil and twist edges to seal. (You can use parchment paper in between the brats and the foil if you wish.)

7 Place in the baking pan covered with aluminum foil in the oven and steam for 45 minutes. Remove from the oven and let rest 30 minutes, if you can.

8 Unwrap the brats and place them in the prepared smoker and smoke for 45 minutes. Enjoy out of the smoker, dry fry in a pan, or grill for additional browning.

SERVES 5

1¼ cups (125 g) vital wheat gluten

¼ cup (15 g) nutritional yeast

1 teaspoon fennel seeds

1 teaspoon granulated garlic

1 teaspoon granulated onion

1 teaspoon rubbed sage

½ teaspoon dry mustard powder

½ teaspoon smoked paprika

½ teaspoon kosher salt

½ teaspoon freshly ground black pepper

¼ teaspoon ground allspice

½ cup (130 g) canned cannellini beans, drained and rinsed

1 tablespoon (15 g) white miso paste

2 tablespoons (30 ml) soy sauce

1 cup (235ml) IPA-style beer

¼ teaspoon liquid smoke

Smoked Trumpet Mushroom Seared "Scallops"

When you want to impress at the dinner table, this recipe will deliver and have you looking like a vegan Gordon whatshisface.

1   To make brown butter, melt 4 tablespoons (55 g) of the butter in a small saucepan over medium heat. Swirl the butter in the pan as it begins to foam and continue to cook for 2 to 3 minutes, until brown specks start to appear in the butter. Remove it from the heat and set aside.

2   Slice the mushrooms into 1-inch (2.5 cm) thick rounds, for twelve total mushroom scallops.

3   Melt the remaining 1 tablespoon (15 g) butter in a large cast-iron skillet over medium-high heat. Add the thyme sprigs and stir them around to add to the flavor of the butter. Add the mushroom scallops. Spoon half of the brown butter over the scallops and cook for 3 to 5 minutes, until the bottoms are golden brown. Flip and spoon the remaining brown butter over the top of each. Cook for 3 to 5 more minutes, until tender.

4   Sprinkle with salt, pepper, and thyme leaves before serving.

SERVES 4

5 tablespoons (70 g) unsalted vegan butter

1 pound (455 g) king trumpet mushrooms (about 2 of the same size)

4 sprigs thyme, plus extra for garnish

Kosher salt

Freshly ground black pepper

Maple-Glazed Tempeh Bacun

Baacccuuuuunnnn! Boy! Bacon was a tough one to give up when making my transition! So I had to find an alternative, fast!! This sweet, salty, savory version will take on those flavors needed to carry the bacon crown! Tempeh is a great sliced meat substitute. It holds up to marinades, and it's healthy!

1 Arrange the tempeh bacon in a single layer in a baking pan.

2 Combine the soy sauce, cider vinegar, olive oil, maple syrup, liquid smoke, smoked paprika, granulated onion, cumin, and salt in a small mixing bowl. Pour the marinade into the baking pan making sure to cover the tempeh. Marinate for at least 2 hours, or overnight.

3 Prepare your smoker for a 1-hour smoke session over low heat.

4 Place the tempeh slices directly on your smoker grate and smoke for a full hour. Remove from the smoker and cool.

SERVES 4

8 ounces (225g) thinly sliced tempeh bacon (Lightlife Organic Tempeh Strips Smoky Fakin Bacon is recommended)

2 tablespoons (30 ml) soy sauce

1 tablespoon (15 ml) apple cider vinegar

1 tablespoon (15 ml) extra-virgin olive oil

1 tablespoon (15 ml) pure maple syrup

½ teaspoon liquid smoke

1 teaspoon smoked paprika

½ teaspoon granulated onion

¼ teaspoon ground cumin

¼ teaspoon kosher salt

Roasted or Steamed Faux Turkey

Christmas, Thanksgiving, New Year's, whatever the holiday is, this faux turkey will provide you with that traditional turkey flavor and texture.

MAKE THE FAUX TURKEY:

1   Combine the chickpeas, water, sesame oil, coconut aminos, soup base, nutritional yeast, poultry seasoning, granulated onion, granulated garlic, black pepper, rosemary, and thyme in a food processor. Process until smooth.

2   Pour the puree into a large bowl, scraping out as much as possible with a spatula. Mix in the vital wheat gluten by hand until combined (it won't stick to your hands). Knead the dough 10 to 15 times, until firm and elastic. Shape into a log.

TO STEAM:

3   Fill the base of a medium pot with steamer insert with the vegetable stock. Place the faux turkey roll into the steamer insert. Cover with the lid and bring to a boil on high heat. Lower the heat to maintain a good simmer and steam for 1 hour. Baste the roast after 30 minutes with a ⅓ cup (80 ml) of the hot stock and add a little more veggie stock if necessary to the bottom of pot.

4   Remove the turkey loaf from the steamer and cool for at least 10 minutes.

SERVES 8

FAUX TURKEY

1 (16-ounce/455 g) can chickpeas, rinsed and drained

¾ cup (175 ml) water

2 tablespoons (30 ml) toasted or regular sesame oil

2 tablespoons (30 ml) coconut aminos (or substitute soy sauce)

1 tablespoon (15 ml) Better Than Bouillon No Chicken soup base

3 tablespoons (10 g) nutritional yeast

½ teaspoon poultry seasoning

1 teaspoon granulated onion

½ teaspoon granulated garlic

¼ teaspoon freshly ground black pepper

½ teaspoon finely chopped fresh rosemary

¼ teaspoon dried thyme

1½ cups (150 g) vital wheat gluten

STEAMING

3 cups (705 ml) vegetable stock

TO BAKE IN THE OVEN:

5   Preheat oven 375°F (190°C). Prepare the baste by combining the melted vegan butter, tamari, and poultry seasoning. Place the whole steamed turkey in a small casserole dish not much bigger than the roast. Pour in the veggie broth (don't add broth until oven is preheated). Brush on the baste. Bake, uncovered, for 35 minutes, basting halfway through. Add splash extra broth, if needed.

6   Slice thinly and serve warm. Or cool completely, refrigerate, and slice as deli meat.

OVEN BAKING

2 tablespoons (30 ml) melted unsalted vegan butter

1 tablespoon (15 ml) tamari or soy sauce

¼ teaspoon poultry seasoning

¾ cup (175 ml) vegetable broth

Smoked TVP Meatball Marinara

This recipe has multiple applications. Meatball subs, pasta, pizza toppings, you name it. Almost as many as Bubba and his shrimp!!

SERVES 4

1 Bring the broth to a boil and pour over the TVP in a large bowl. Cover and allow to sit for 10 minutes until completely absorbed.

2 Add the granulated onion, granulated garlic, Italian seasoning, Worcestershire sauce, nutritional yeast, and flour. Combine into a thick dough that holds together when squeezed in your palm. Depending on the type of flour you use, you may need to add a bit extra. If needed, add an additional 1 tablespoon flour at a time. Stir thoroughly after each addition. Add salt and pepper as needed, depending on whether the broth and Italian seasoning contain salt.

3 Preheat the oven to 400°F (200°C).

4 Shape the mixture into 1- to 2-inch (2.5 to 5 cm) balls. Combine with the tomato puree in a baking dish and top with the vegan mozzarella.

5 Bake for 20 minutes. Meanwhile, prepare your smoker for a 20-minute smoke session (85°–120°F [30°–50°C]).

6 Remove the pan from the oven and head straight to your smoker. Smoke for 20 minutes. Serve right out of the smoker.

⅞ cup (205 ml) vegetable broth (1 cup minus 2 tablespoons)

1 cup (100 g) TVP (textured soy protein)

1 teaspoon granulated onion

1 teaspoon granulated garlic

2 teaspoons Italian seasoning

1 tablespoon (15 ml) vegan Worcestershire sauce or soy sauce

2 tablespoons (10 g) nutritional yeast

¼ cup (30 g) all-purpose flour or dried breadcrumbs, plus more as needed

Kosher salt and freshly ground black pepper

4 cups (950 ml) canned tomato puree

2 cups (230 g) shredded vegan mozzarella

5

Veggie
Forward

Smoked Watermelon Poke Bowl

This is actually a recipe I picked up along my travels. You couldn't tell me that this wasn't actually ahi tuna! The texture, the flavor, it was unreal! So I had to try it myself, but I wanted to add a little Southern flare and smoke to it! Serve with white or brown rice.

1   Combine the lemon zest, ginger, maple syrup, cayenne, and salt into a mixing bowl. Add the lemon juice, rice vinegar, soy sauce, and liquid smoke and whisk until blended. While still whisking, slowly pour in the olive and sesame oils and continue whisking until incorporated

2   Add the watermelon cubes to the marinade and toss until coated. Transfer the watermelon and marinade to a lidded storage container and store in fridge for at least 4 hours, or overnight.

3   Remove the watermelon from the marinade with slotted spoon or strain with strainer.

4   Put rice in each serving bowl and top with a generous amount of the marinated watermelon.

5   Garnish with sesame seeds and scallions. Serve at once.

Note   You can also add red onion, broccoli, carrots, or any other vegetable you can think of to a poke bowl.

SERVES 4

Finely grated zest of 1 medium lemon

1 teaspoon fresh grated ginger

1 tablespoon (30 ml) pure maple syrup

¾ teaspoon cayenne pepper

1 teaspoon kosher salt

1 tablespoon (15 ml) fresh lemon juice

¼ cup (60 ml) rice wine vinegar

⅓ cup (80 ml) soy sauce

1 teaspoon liquid smoke

2 tablespoons (30 ml) extra-virgin olive oil

2 tablespoons (30 ml) sesame oil

3 pounds (1.5 kg) seedless watermelon flesh, cut into 1.2-inch (1 cm) cubes

Cooked white or brown rice, to serve

Black sesame seeds, to serve

Chopped scallions, white and green parts, to serve

Smoked Stout Beer Baked Beans

I don't think I've been to a barbecue or cookout without there being some variation of baked beans. The sweet molasses kissed with a hint of smokiness can become an intoxicating concoction! The goal with this one was to create a version that provides you with that cured bacon smoke without the slaughter. I think we got it!

1 Preheat the oven to 375°F (190°C).

2 Heat the oil over medium heat in a large heavy Dutch oven. Add the onion and sauté until tender and beginning to brown, about 5 minutes. Add the beer, barbecue sauce, brown sugar, cider vinegar, molasses, mustard, beans, vegan bacon, salt, pepper, and liquid smoke. Bring the mixture to a simmer. Stir in the apple and cover the pot with the lid or aluminum foil.

3 Bake for at least an hour, until the beans are thick, smooth, and bubbly, adding additional beer if it gets too thick. (You can substitute apple juice if you don't want to add more of the beer.)

4 Take that pan of deliciousness from the oven to the table and serve piping hot.

SERVES 4

2 tablespoons (30 ml) vegetable oil

1 medium onion, diced or chopped

2 cups (475 ml) Guinness or other stout beer, plus more if needed

¾ cup (175 ml) Smoky Vidalia VBQ sauce (see recipe, page 38)

2 tablespoons (30 g) packed light brown sugar

2 tablespoons (30 ml) apple cider vinegar

2 tablespoons (30 ml) molasses

2 tablespoons (20 g) Dijon mustard

4 cups (1 kg) cooked white northern beans

½ cup (55 g) chopped vegan bacon or bacon bits

½ teaspoon kosher salt

1 teaspoon freshly ground black pepper

2 tablespoons (30 ml) liquid smoke

1 medium Granny Smith apple, peeled and diced

Smoked Sundried Tomato Tapenade

This Mediterranean dish is a versatile condiment. It works particularly well as a complement to a vegan cheese board.

Mix together the olives, sun dried tomatoes, capers, and fresh herbs. Add the garlic, lemon juice, salt, pepper, and red pepper flakes. Drizzle in the olive oil and stir. Taste and adjust for lemon juice and garlic. Serve at room temperature.

SERVES 4

2 cups (280 g) pitted olives (mix of black, green and kalamata), finely chopped

¼ cup (15 g) smoked sun dried tomatoes, finely chopped

2 tablespoons (15 g) capers, finely chopped

¼ cup (15 g) chopped fresh flat-leaf parsley leaves, finely chopped

8 to 10 basil leaves, finely chopped

1 clove garlic, minced

Juice of ½ fresh lemon, plus more if needed

½ teaspoon Kosher salt

Freshly ground black pepper

½ teaspoon red pepper flakes

¼ cup (60 ml) extra-virgin olive oil, plus more if needed

Glazed Smoked Asparagus

I always serve this in the spring, when asparagus is at its peak freshness.

1   Preheat a grill for direct grilling.

2   In a shallow dish, whisk the mayonnaise with the oil, lemon juice, agave syrup, garlic, paprika, salt, and coriander. Add the asparagus and toss; let stand for 30 minutes.

3   Grill the asparagus over moderately high heat, turning, until tender and blistered in spots, 6 minutes. Serve.

SERVES 4

½ cup (115 g) vegan mayonnaise

¼ cup (60 ml) extra-virgin olive oil

3 tablespoons (45 ml) fresh lemon juice

1 teaspoon agave syrup

1 clove garlic, crushed

1 tablespoon (10 g) smoked paprika

2 teaspoons kosher salt

1 teaspoon coriander seeds

1 pound (455 g) thick asparagus, trimmed

Smoky Collard Greens

A Southern classic! This dish has to be done right, for grandmother's sake.

1   Taking several collard leaves at once, stack them and then roll the stack into a tight cigar shape. Slice the rolled collard greens into thin strips. Repeat until you've cut all the greens.

2   In a small bowl, mix together the soy sauce, maple syrup, hot sauce, and liquid smoke.

3   Heat a large skillet over medium heat. Add 1 teaspoon of the oil, and then add the collard greens and a pinch of salt. Cook for 3 to 5 minutes, stirring occasionally, until the collard greens are wilted, tender, and bright green.

4   Move the collards over so they only cover about half the pan. In the empty space, add the remaining 2 teaspoons of oil and the sliced garlic. Cook the garlic in oil, stirring, for 60 to 90 seconds, until it is lightly golden. Then stir everything together.

5   Add the soy sauce mixture to the greens and cook for another minute or so, until the sauce is thick and absorbed. Taste and add salt, if desired. Remove from the heat and serve.

SERVES 4

1 large bunch collard greens, tough stems removed

2 tablespoons (30 ml) soy sauce or tamari

2 teaspoons pure maple syrup

1 teaspoon Tabasco sauce or other hot sauce

½ teaspoon liquid smoke

1 tablespoon (15 ml) vegetable oil

Kosher salt

2 cloves garlic, thinly sliced

Grilled Sweet Glazed Carrots

A smoky riff on a family-friendly classic, these are always on my menu when kids are around.

1 Preheat a grill for direct and indirect cooking.

2 Make the glaze: Combine the butter, brown sugar, honey, and salt and mix together. For additional flavor, add the orange juice and cinnamon. Whisk frequently until the brown sugar dissolves. Keep warm.

3 Toss carrots in the olive oil, then place directly on the grill over low heat. Rotate every few minutes to get a slight char on each side, 12 to 15 minutes. If the carrots begin to burn, move them to indirect heat. Just before pulling the carrots off the grill, glaze them once. Let them cook 1 more minute on the grill, then remove from grill and glaze one more time. Serve immediately.

SERVES 4

2 tablespoons (30 g) vegan butter

¼ cup (60 g) packed light brown sugar

¼ cup (60 ml) honey

⅛ teaspoon kosher salt

1 tablespoon (15 ml) fresh orange juice (optional)

¼ teaspoon ground cinnamon (optional)

1 pound (455 g) carrots

1 tablespoon (15 ml) extra-virgin olive oil

VBQ Green Beans

Green beans can be boring on their own, but this preparation surrounds them in a symphony of intense flavorings.

1   Preheat the oven to 350°F (180°C).

2   Fry the bacon bits in dry skillet over medium-high heat until golden brown.

3   Remove the cooked bacon (leaving grease in skillet) and set aside. Add the onions and garlic to the skillet and cook over low heat until translucent, about 4 to 7 minutes. Add the barbecue sauce, ketchup, Worcestershire sauce, brown sugar, and cayenne. Stir and cook together until golden brown, about 3 to 4 minutes. Stir half of the bacon bits into sauce.

4   Combine the green beans and sauce in a small, square baking dish. Toss and stir to coat.

5   Bake for about 15 minutes. Top with remaining bacon pieces and serve.

SERVES 4

3 to 4 ounces (85 to 113 g) tempeh bacon (Lightlife Organic Tempeh Strips Smoky Fakin Bacon is recommended), cut in bite-size pieces

1 medium onion, diced

2 teaspoons minced garlic

½ cup (120 ml) Smoky Vidalia VBQ sauce (see recipe, page 38)

2 tablespoons (30 ml) ketchup

1 tablespoon (15 ml) vegan Worcestershire sauce

1½ tablespoons (20 g) packed light brown sugar

¼ teaspoon cayenne pepper (optional)

30 ounces (850 g) fresh green beans

Southern Fried Cabbage

The name speaks for itself. We fry everything in the South! From our food to our hair, something is hitting the grease.

1   Fry the bacon in a medium dry skillet for about 3 to 5 minutes until golden brown. Coarsely chop the bacon.

2   Melt the vegan butter in the same skillet over medium-low heat. Add the onion and cook until tender, 3 to 4 minutes. Add the chopped bacon to the skillet and stir to combine with the butter and onions. Add the cabbage and cook until tender, stirring several times to make sure it does not burn and that it cooks evenly, 5 to 7 minutes. Season to taste with salt, pepper and, if desired, Cajun seasoning and red pepper flakes. Serve hot.

SERVES 4

6 slices tempeh bacon (Lightlife Organic Tempeh Strips Smoky Fakin Bacon is recommended)

2 tablespoons (30 g) vegan butter

1 medium onion, chopped

1 head green cabbage, cored and thinly sliced

Kosher salt and pepper

¼ to ½ teaspoon Cajun seasoning (optional)

¼ teaspoon red pepper flakes (optional)

Intense Kimchi

I've always been a fan of Asian cuisine. Especially those dishes that go back centuries. This kimchi recipe was gifted to me by a good friend of mine. I have replaced the fish sauce with our own vegan version.

Make sure that you are using clean surfaces and utensils and are washing your hands throughout the process of preparing your kimchi in order to prevent introducing bad bacteria and disrupting the fermentation process. The photos provide step-by-step instructions, so if you get lost, refer back to those.

PREPARE THE CABBAGE:

1 Quarter the cabbage and carefully remove the bottom core (hard white section) with a sharp knife. Discard. Transfer the cabbage into a large mixing bowl and begin packing a generous amount of salt in between each of the leaves. Do so by lifting each individual leaf and sprinkling with salt. Repeat until all leaves have been salted. Then press down and let rest for 30 minutes. This softens and breaks down the cabbage, drawing out moisture, priming it to be coated in the sauce.

MAKE THE VEGAN FISH SAUCE:

2 Combine the tamari, coconut oil, pineapple juice, and water in a small mixing bowl and whisk to blend. Set aside.

continued

SERVES 4

CABBAGE

1 head napa or savoy cabbage, outermost leaves removed

1 tablespoon (10 g) kosher salt, plus more as needed

VEGAN FISH SAUCE

2 tablespoons (30 ml) tamari

2 tablespoons (30 g) coconut oil

¼ cup (60 ml) pineapple juice

¼ cup (60 ml) warm water

continued

MAKE THE CHILE SAUCE:

3 Combine the ginger, garlic, and onion in a food processor or blender. Add 3 to 4 tablespoons (10 to 15 g) of the chili flakes and process until blended. If you desire more heat, continue to add chili flakes by the tablespoon (5 g). I use ½ cup (30 g) chile flakes so it is quite spicy, as I prefer. Add the vegan fish sauce to this mixture and pulse to combine. Set aside.

4 At this time, your cabbage should be ready to flip. Wash your hands and turn each section of cabbage over so it's facing the opposite direction. Then pack down with your hands to compress. Repeat this process three more times, waiting 30 minutes in between each flip, and washing your hands before touching the cabbage.

PREPARE THE VEGETABLES:

5 Combine the carrots and green onion, if using, in a medium mixing bowl, along with the sauce. Stir to combine, then cover and set aside.

6 While waiting, sterilize your storage containers. Bring a pot of water to a boil and place your containers (I used 1 large mason jar, and 1 small glass container) in a clean sink and pour the boiling water over top. Let containers cool slightly, then dry with a clean towel and set aside.

7 Once you have flipped your cabbage four times (it should be tender and shrunken down quite a bit), it's time to rinse. In very cold water, rinse each section of cabbage to remove excess salt, then place on two or three absorbent, clean towels and pat dry. Also separate the cabbage leaves at this time, so they're easier to work with.

CHILE SAUCE

3 tablespoons (20 g) minced fresh ginger

1 head garlic, cloves separated and peeled

1 small white onion, quartered

Korean chili flakes

VEGETABLES

2 carrots, finely chopped or cut into matchsticks, a.k.a. Julienned

6 scallions, white and green parts, coarsely chopped (optional)

8   Rinse and dry the mixing bowl the cabbage was in, then return the cabbage to the bowl. Begin coating each leaf with the sauce you set aside. If you have gloves (disposable or rubber), use them at this time as the sauce can irritate sensitive hands (I didn't, but thought it was worth mentioning). Be generous when coating, but also keep in mind you need enough sauce to coat all of the cabbage. Once the cabbage is thoroughly coated with sauce, wash your hands and set out your sterilized storage containers.

9   With clean hands, begin placing the coated cabbage leaves in the container, packing down to ensure there is as little air as possible between leaves. Continue until all cabbage is packed in, then press down very firmly to remove air. Top the containers with clean, sterilized lids, and set in a cool dark place (such as a cabinet, not the refrigerator) to ferment.

10 Each day it ferments, open up the jars and press down with a clean utensil, such as a spoon, to press out air bubbles and ensure the kimchi is immersed in liquid. A good sign of proper fermentation is seeing little bubbles in the sauce when you press down.

11 How long to ferment is up to you. The resource I used suggested 36 hours minimum, then transfer to the refrigerator for 1 week to ferment longer. I fermented mine for about 48 hours. But next time I think I'll ferment for 1 week for softer cabbage and a more intense fermented flavor. The longer you ferment the kimchi, the tangier and more intense the flavor will be, and the more tender the cabbage will become. From what I've read, I wouldn't ferment for more than 21 days. A good indicator of when it's done fermenting is the smell. If it smells pleasant to the nose and tangy, like the kimchi you're used to trying, it's probably ready to transfer to the refrigerator.

12 Kimchi will keep in the refrigerator for at least 3 to 4 weeks, and even months. You'll know it's gone bad if mold has formed or the smell is sour or unpleasant.

Grilled Smoked Vegetable Kabobs

A barbecue staple. These are always a hit at the many different functions we cater. We kick it up a bit with a smoked butter to finish. Healthy? Maybe! For this recipe, you will need to soak eight to twelve 8-inch (20-cm) wooden skewers in water for 15 to 30 minutes.

1   Skewer the vegetables by alternating between red onion, zucchini, and the different colored bell peppers. Brush the veggies with a light layer of olive oil.

2   Prepare the smoker for a 60-minute smoke session over low heat.

3   Smoke the vegetables for 60 minutes. Remove from the smoker, brush with the smoked butter, and drizzle with balsamic vinegar, if desired. Enjoy!

SERVES 4

4 medium red onions, halved

4 medium zucchini, sliced into rounds

2 red bell peppers, seeded and chopped into 1-inch (2.5 cm) squares

2 orange bell peppers, seeded and chopped into 1-inch (2.5 cm) squares

2 yellow bell peppers, seeded and chopped into 1-inch (2.5 cm) squares

2 green bell peppers, seeded and chopped into 1-inch (2.5 cm) squares

1 large eggplant, sliced into rounds

Extra-virgin olive oil

2 cups (467 g) Roasted Garlic Smoked Butta (see recipe, page 28)

Balsamic vinegar (optional)

Prickly B&B Pickles

Pickles, pickles, pickles! Sweet, tangy, spicy! Pickles are a labor of love—and a de rigueur accompaniment for barbecue. These are "quick pickles" or "refrigerator pickles," which means you do not process them for canning, which makes them much easier to prepare.

1   Combine the cucumbers and salt in a large, shallow bowl; cover and chill for 1½ hours. Transfer the cucumbers to a colander and rinse thoroughly under cold water. Drain well, and return the cucumbers to bowl. Add the onion to the bowl.

2   Combine the white sugar, white vinegar, cider vinegar, brown sugar, mustard seeds, celery seeds, turmeric, and red pepper flakes in a medium saucepan; bring to a simmer over medium heat, stirring until sugar dissolves. Pour the hot vinegar mixture over the cucumber mixture; let stand at room temperature for 1 hour. Cover and refrigerate for 24 hours.

3   Store in an airtight container in refrigerator up to 2 weeks.

SERVES 4

5½ cups (1½ pounds/680 g) ½-inch (1 cm) sliced pickling cucumbers

1½ tablespoons (15 g) kosher salt

1 cup (115 g) thinly sliced sweet onion

1 cup (200 g) granulated white sugar

1 cup (235 ml) distilled white vinegar

½ cup (120 ml) apple cider vinegar

¼ cup (60 g) packed light brown sugar

1½ teaspoons mustard seeds

½ teaspoon celery seeds

⅛ teaspoon ground turmeric

1 teaspoon red pepper flakes

Smoky Cowboy Caviar

Your typical cowboy probably never heard of caviar.
But the cowboys' own version is just as classy and just as
tasty — and a lot less expensive.

Combine the black beans, black-eyed peas, onion, corn, avocado, tomatoes, cilantro, jalapeño, olive oil, lime juice, liquid smoke, cumin, and chili powder in a medium mixing bowl. Toss until combined and coated. Season to taste with salt and pepper and serve.

SERVES 4

1 (15-ounce/425 g) can black beans, drained and rinsed

1 cup (180 g) canned black-eyed peas

½ red onion, diced

1 cup (180 g) corn, canned and drained

1 avocado, peeled, pitted, and diced

2 plum tomatoes (Roma), diced

¼ cup (5 g) chopped fresh cilantro

1 jalapeño, seeded and finely chopped

¼ cup (60 ml) extra-virgin olive oil

Juice of 1 lime

1 teaspoon liquid smoke

½ teaspoon ground cumin

½ teaspoon chili powder

Kosher salt and freshly ground pepper

Smoky Creamy Pumpkin Soup

Some people find that pumpkin without a lot of sugar added (as in a pumpkin pie) is too pungent or bitter. Here the mild sweetness of the sweet potatoes does the trick, taking the edge off the assertive flavor of pumpkin.

1   Heat the onion and olive oil in a Dutch oven or large pot over medium heat. Cook until the onion is softened, 5 to 8 minutes, stirring occasionally. Add the sweet potato, pumpkin, tomato sauce, honey, if using, vegetable stock, liquid smoke, granulated garlic, cinnamon, and salt, stirring to combine.

2   Cover, bring to a boil, then reduce the heat to a simmer and cook until the sweet potatoes are very tender, 25 to 30 minutes.

3   Transfer the soup to a food processor and process until smooth. Serve hot, garnished with vegan sour cream.

SERVES 4

1 medium yellow onion, finely chopped

1 tablespoon (15 ml) extra-virgin olive oil

2 cups (265 g) peeled, chopped sweet potato

2 (15-ounce/425 g) cans pumpkin puree

1 (15-ounce/425 g) can unseasoned tomato sauce

2 teaspoons honey (optional)

4 cups (950 ml) vegetable stock

1 teaspoon liquid smoke

1 teaspoon granulated garlic

1 teaspoon ground cinnamon

1½ teaspoons kosher salt

Vegan sour cream, to garnish

Crisp Carrot Chips with Smoky Pomegranate Ketchup

It's incredible what a healthy dose of pomegranate molasses will do to a simple serving of bottled ketchup.

1   Using a vegetable peeler, cut thick ribbons (press down hard to get thick ribbons) from the carrots.

2   Heat the oil to 360°F (180°C) in a deep saucepan over high heat. Fry the carrot ribbons, a few at a time, until crispy and lightly browned (they will continue to crisp up once they cool down). Sprinkle with salt.

3   To make the pomegranate ketchup, stir together the ketchup, pomegranate molasses, and liquid smoke. Serve with the carrot ribbons for dipping. Store extra ketchup in a mason jar or airtight container in the refrigerator for 2 to 3 weeks.

SERVES 4

3 medium carrots

Canola oil, for frying

Kosher salt

½ cup (120 g) ketchup

¼ cup (60 ml) pomegranate molasses

1 teaspoon liquid smoke

Loaded VBQ Nachos

Another one of our menu items that flies! This version combines the smokiness from the barbecue sauce and the meaty umami from the shredded jackfruit to give you an authentic barbecue flare.

1   Preheat the oven to 350°F (180°C).

2   Heat the olive oil and jackfruit in a skillet over medium heat until heated through. Sauté for 5 to 7 minutes. Add the barbecue sauce and cook for 5 to 6 minutes.

3   Spread out the tortilla chips in a cast-iron skillet or on a baking sheet and bake in the oven for 5 to 6 minutes, until warm.

4   Remove the chips from the oven and top with the jackfruit mixture, black beans, bell pepper, cherry tomatoes, onions, cilantro, the remaining 2 tablespoons (30 ml) barbecue sauce, and any other toppings you desire. Serve and enjoy!

SERVES 4

2 tablespoons (30 ml) extra-virgin olive oil

1 (20-ounce/565 g) can young jackfruit, drained, rinsed, and shredded

⅓ cup (80 ml) plus 2 tablespoons (30 ml) Smoky Vidalia VBQ Sauce (see recipe, page 38)

1 12-ounce (340 g) bag of tortilla chips

½ (15-ounce/440 g) can black beans, drained and rinsed

½ red bell pepper, diced

1 cup (150g) cherry tomatoes, halved

⅓ cup (55 g) chopped red onions

3 tablespoons (50 g) chopped cilantro

Additional toppings: vegan sour cream, salsa, chopped jalapeño, vegan queso

Loaded Mashed Potato Casserole

I loooove mashed potatoes! This casserole is an amazing vegan spin on the timeless nonvegan version.

1   Bring a large pot of water to a boil; add 2 tablespoons (20 g) of kosher salt. Add the potatoes to the pot and boil for 15 to 20 minutes, until the potatoes are tender.

2   Drain the potatoes. Run the potatoes through a ricer and return them to the pot. Alternatively, you can skip the ricing step and simply mash the potatoes with a potato masher or mixer.

3   Stir in the oat milk, vegan butter, and vegan sour cream. Add salt and pepper to taste. Stir in 1 cup (120 g) of the vegan cheese.

4   Preheat the oven to 350°F (180°C). Coat a 9-inch (23-cm) square pan or 2-quart (2-L) casserole dish with cooking spray.

5   Transfer the potatoes to the prepared baking dish. Top with the remaining ⅔ cup (70 g) cheese. Cover the pan with foil.

6   Bake for 20 minutes. Remove the foil and add the bacon; bake, uncovered for an additional 20 minutes or until cheese is bubbly and potatoes are heated through.

7   Sprinkle the chives and parsley over the top and serve.

SERVES 4

3 pounds (1.5 kg) russet potatoes, peeled and cut into 1½-inch (5 cm) pieces

¾ cup (175 ml) unsweetened oat milk

¼ cup (55 g) vegan unsalted butter, melted

1 cup (230 g) vegan sour cream

Kosher salt and freshly ground black pepper

1⅔ cups (190 g) shredded vegan cheddar cheese

½ cup (120 ml) crumbled cooked tempeh bacon (Lightlife Organic Tempeh Strips Smoky Fakin Bacon is recommended)

¼ cup (10 g) finely chopped fresh chives

2 tablespoons (10 g) finely chopped flat-leaf parsley

Smoked Corn and Potato Hash

I love this dish! The heartiness of the ingredients makes this a great heat-and-eat meal in itself!

Heat a large, heavy skillet over medium-high heat. Add the olive oil and potatoes and toss well to coat. Stir occasionally to prevent sticking and let them soften and brown slightly, 7 to 8 minutes. Add the corn, bacon, and onion. Continue to stir and let them begin to brown slightly, 7 to 8 minutes. Add the parsley, vegan butter, liquid smoke, salt, and pepper. Stir to combine. Serve hot.

SERVES 4

1 tablespoon (15 ml) extra-virgin olive oil

2 cups (220 g) diced red potatoes (½-inch/1 cm dice)

1 cup (140g) fresh or frozen and thawed corn kernels

1 tablespoon (19 g) chopped tempeh bacon (Lightlife Organic Tempeh Strips Smoky Fakin Bacon is recommended)

½ cup (40 g) diced yellow onion

½ cup (30 g) chopped fresh flat-leaf parsley

2 tablespoons (30 g) unsalted vegan butter

1 teaspoon liquid smoke

1 teaspoon kosher salt

½ teaspoon freshly ground black pepper

Mushroom Risotto

One of my favorite dishes in the whole wide world! But risotto is often difficult to make. Risotto is a labor of love and this one screams "I Love You!"

1   Combine the vegan butter and miso in a small bowl and use a fork to cream them together until well combined.

2   Heat the vegetable broth in a saucepan over medium-high heat. Once it comes to a simmer, adjust the heat to keep the broth warm at a gentle simmer.

3   To cook the mushrooms, heat a large nonstick frying pan over medium-high heat and add 1 tablespoon (15 ml) of the olive oil. Once shimmering, add the mushrooms. Allow to cook undisturbed for a few minutes to develop some browning. Continue to cook for a total of 8 to 9 minutes, until the mushrooms are nicely browned, stirring only occasionally. Add the thyme and half of the garlic to the mushrooms. Season with ½ teaspoon kosher salt. Cook for 2 to 4 minutes until golden brown, stirring frequently to prevent burning.

4   Add the creamed miso butter to the pan and stir into the mushrooms. Season with a pinch of salt and pepper and cook for 2 more minutes. Turn off the heat and set the mushrooms aside.

5   To cook the risotto, heat a large nonstick saucepan or deep sauté pan over medium heat. Add the remaining 2 tablespoons (30 ml) of olive oil. Once hot, add the leeks and remaining garlic and cook for 2 to 3 minutes, until the leeks have just softened.

continued

SERVES 4

¼ cup (55 g) vegan butter, at room temperature

2 tablespoons (30 g) white miso paste

6 to 8 cups (1.5 to 2 L) vegetable broth

3 tablespoons (45 ml) extra-virgin olive oil

20 ounces (565 g) mixed fresh mushrooms, sliced

2 tablespoons (5 g) coarsely chopped fresh thyme leaves

6 cloves garlic, minced

2 large leeks, white and pale green parts only, diced

½ teaspoon kosher salt, plus more to taste

Freshly cracked black pepper

2 cups (390 g) arborio rice

⅔ cup (160 ml) white wine

¼ cup (25 g) grated vegan Parmesan cheese (optional)

1 handful fresh Italian flat-leaf parsley, chopped

6   Add the rice and stir quickly until all of the rice grains are well-coated and the rice smells slightly toasty, 60 to 90 seconds. Pour in the wine and stir to scrape any bits stuck to the bottom of the pot, cooking until the wine has nearly all evaporated, 3 to 4 minutes.

7   Ladle in 1 cup (235 ml) of the warm vegetable broth and stir frequently but not constantly. When the rice has absorbed the liquid, add the next round of broth, 1 cup (235 ml) at a time. Continue this process stirring about every 30 seconds and adding more broth when most of the liquid is absorbed, for about 20 minutes, until the risotto is slightly firm and creamy, but not too soft or mushy.

8   To test for doneness, you can place the rice on a flat surface and smear downwards with your finger. It should be fairly smooth, but you should still be able to see a bit of the white, the al dente center of the rice.

9   Transfer the cooked miso mushrooms to the risotto and stir to warm through for a few minutes. Remove from the heat, and then stir in vegan Parmesan cheese, if using. Taste for seasonings, adding a bit of salt as needed and some black pepper to season. Garnish with fresh chopped parsley and serve immediately.

Smoky Ratatouille

A classic French Provençale dish that tastes even better when the veggies are grilled, as here, and that can be the ultimate dinner meat substitute.

1   Heat the olive oil in a 12-inch (30 cm) cast-iron skillet. Add the onion, garlic, and bell peppers and sauté until soft. Season with salt and pepper, then add the crushed tomatoes. Stir until ingredients are fully incorporated.

2   Turn off the heat, then add basil. Stir once more, then smooth the surface of the sauce with your spatula or spoon.

3   Arrange the sliced veggies in overlapping pattern on top of the sauce from the outer edge to the inside of the pan. Season with salt and pepper and sprinkle the parsley and thyme over the top.

4   Set the temperature of your grill to 180°F (80°C) and preheat with the lid closed for 15 minutes.

5   Place the pan on grill grate and smoke for 10 minutes. Then cover pan with foil and increase the grill temperature to 375°F (190°C) and cook for 40 minutes.

6   After 40 minutes, remove the foil, sprinkle a generous amount of Parmesan cheese on top. Continue to cook for an additional 20 minutes, or until the vegetables are soft and the cheese is melted.

7   Remove from the grill and sprinkle more cheese over top and sprinkle with fresh parsley. Serve immediately with your favorite sides, such as bread or salad. Enjoy!

SERVES 4

2 tablespoons (30 ml) extra-virgin olive oil

1 medium yellow onion, diced

6 cloves garlic, minced

2 red or green bell peppers, diced

Kosher salt and freshly ground black pepper

1 (28-ounce/790 g) can crushed tomatoes

¼ cup (10 g) chopped fresh basil

2 eggplants, sliced into ¼-inch (5-mm) rounds

6 plum (Roma) tomatoes, sliced into ¼-inch (5-mm) rounds

2 yellow squash, sliced into ¼-inch (5-mm) rounds

2 zucchinis, sliced into ¼-inch (5-mm) rounds

1 teaspoon minced garlic

2 tablespoons (10 g) chopped fresh flat-leaf parsley, plus more to garnish

2 teaspoons chopped fresh thyme leaves

Vegan Parmesan cheese, grated

Smoked Rutabaga Gratin

Rutabagas are the cousin of the turnip. Creating this gratin showed me that the rutabaga makes a great dish.

1 To prepare the rutabagas on the stovetop, put them in a large saucepan. Cover with water and bring to a boil. Lower the heat and simmer, uncovered, for 35 to 40 minutes, until the rutabagas are fork tender.

2 In the meantime, prepare the cashew cream. Drain the soaked cashews and combine them in a blender with the water and granulated onion. Blend on high speed until smooth, about 1 minute. Set aside.

3 Drain the cooked rutabaga and transfer to a food processor. Process for 5 to 7 seconds, until it has the texture of slightly chunky mashed potatoes; don't overprocess.

4 Transfer the pureed rutabaga to a large mixing bowl. Add the molasses, cashew cream, salt, ginger, nutmeg, cinnamon, and white pepper. Using a wooden spoon or spatula, mix to combine. Once fully combined, taste and adjust the saltiness to your liking.

5 Preheat the oven to 325°F (170°C). Transfer the rutabaga mixture to a baking dish and smooth the top with a spatula. Sprinkle the breadcrumbs evenly on top. Use a spoon to make a pattern on top of the gratin, if desired.

6 Bake for 1 hour, until the top is golden brown. Let cool a few minutes before serving.

SERVES 6

3 rutabaga, peeled and diced into ½-inch (1 cm) cubes

¾ cup (95 g) raw cashews, covered in water and soaked overnight

1 cup (240 ml) water

1 teaspoon granulated onion

¼ cup (60 ml) molasses

½ teaspoon kosher salt, plus more as needed

½ teaspoon ground ginger

¼ teaspoon ground nutmeg

¼ teaspoon ground cinnamon

¼ teaspoon ground white pepper

⅓ cup (38 g) dried breadcrumbs

Creamy Mushroom Stroganoff

One of my go-to supper dishes for company, especially when I am serving carnivores who are used to bold umami flavors.

1   Heat a large sauté pan with deep sides (or a Dutch oven) over medium-high heat and add 1½ to 2 tablespoons (25 to 30 ml) of the olive oil. Once the oil is shimmering, add half of the leeks and half of the mushrooms. Cook for 8 to 10 minutes, until mushrooms are nicely browned, stirring occasionally. Reduce the heat to medium and add half of the garlic, half of the thyme, and ¼ teaspoon of the salt. Cook for 2 to 4 minutes, until the mushrooms are browned and crispy. Transfer this batch to a plate or bowl and set aside. Repeat the process with the remaining oil, mushrooms, leeks, garlic, thyme, and salt.

2   While the mushrooms are cooking, make the "vegetable broth roux." In a medium bowl, whisk together the vegetable broth, coconut aminos, and flour. Whisk until no clumps remain.

3   Pour the white wine into the pan with the cooked mushrooms, and use a wooden spoon or flat-ended spatula to deglaze the pan by scraping up any brown bits on the bottom of the pan. Lower the heat as needed to simmer for 3 minutes, or until the smell of alcohol has dissipated and the wine has mostly evaporated.

4   Pour the vegetable broth roux into the pan and whisk to combine, ensuring there are no clumps. Bring to a simmer, then pour in the coconut milk, tahini, nutritional yeast, ½ teaspoon salt, and paprika. Bring to a simmer over medium-low heat. Cook for 10 minutes, until the sauce is thickened and very creamy.

5   Meanwhile, cook the pasta. Bring a large saucepan of salted water to a boil. Cook the pasta according to the package instructions until al dente. Drain and keep warm.

6   Stir the mustard into the stroganoff sauce and stir. Add the hot cooked pasta and chopped dill and toss to coat.

7   Divide the pasta among plates or bowls and top each with a spoonful of the first batch of crispy mushrooms and extra dill or pepper to garnish.

SERVES 4

3 to 4 tablespoons (45 to 60 ml) extra-virgin olive oil

2 large leeks or 3 small to medium leeks, white and pale green parts only, sliced

20 ounces (565 g) mixed fresh mushrooms, sliced

6 garlic cloves, minced

1 tablespoon (3 g) coarsely chopped fresh thyme leaves

Kosher salt

1½ cups (355 ml) vegetable broth

2 tablespoons (30 ml) coconut amino

¼ cup (30 g) all-purpose flour

½ cup (120 ml) dry white wine

1 (14-ounce/425 ml) can full-fat coconut milk

2 tablespoons (30 g) tahini

2 tablespoons (10 g) nutritional yeast

1 teaspoon smoked paprika

12 ounces (340 g) pasta

½ teaspoon Dijon mustard

¼ cup (15 g) chopped fresh dill, plus more to garnish

Freshly cracked black pepper

6

Cheesy Things

Smoky Beer Queso Dip

Cheese was definitely one of the last things to go during my vegan journey. I could never find a vegan cheese I liked so I started making my own. This is actually a recipe I use at the restaurant for our smoked bratwurst sandwich. Always a game changer. Pairs well with your favorite raw fruit and vegetables.

1 Combine the cashews, garlic, yeast, cumin, chili powder, salt, liquid smoke, salsa, and beer in a blender. Add ½ cup (120 ml) of the hot oat milk and blend. The better the blender speed, the smoother consistency of your dip. Add additional hot oat milk slowly as needed to get a smooth and creamy texture. If it gets too thin, add more cashews. Too thick, add more oat milk.

2 Season to taste with salt or more chili powder to give it more of a kick. Make it your own!

SERVES 6

1 cup (150 g) raw cashews, plus more if needed

1 clove garlic

3 tablespoons (10 g) nutritional yeast

½ teaspoon ground cumin

1 teaspoon chili powder, plus more if needed

2 teaspoons kosher salt, plus more if needed

1 teaspoon liquid smoke

1 tablespoon (15 ml) your favorite salsa or Ro-tel tomatoes with chiles

¼ cup (60 ml) IPA beer (any brand will do)

1 cup (235 ml) unsweetened oat milk, hot

Smoked Mac 'n' Cheeze

Our signature dish at the shop! The smoke really drives through the entire dish and combines beautifully with the smooth cheese sauce.

1   Preheat the oven to 375°F (190°C).

2   Bring a large pot of salted water to a rolling boil for the pasta. Carefully scoop out a cup of water and pour it into a smaller bowl over your cashews. Soak the cashews for 15 minutes until soft.

3   Cook the pasta for 7 minutes, until al dente (or according to the package directions for al dente). You don't want your pasta to be fully cooked, as it will continue to cook as it bakes. Drain and set aside.

4   Stir together the granulated garlic, granulated onion, chili powder, paprika, and salt in a small bowl.

5   Drain the cashews and transfer to a blender or food processor. Add in the mixed spices, nutritional yeast, and 2 cups (475 ml) of the oat milk. Blend on high speed until creamy. Add the remaining cup (235 ml) of oat milk and blend again. The mixture will be thin, but this is correct!

6   Toss the pasta with the vegan cheese sauce and vegan mozzarella, then pour the mixture into a large rectangular baking pan. Set aside.

7   To make the breadcrumb topping, heat the vegan butter in a small saucepan over medium heat. Add in panko breadcrumbs and thyme and cook for 2 to 3 minutes until fragrant and lightly golden. Sprinkle over the macaroni.

8   Bake for 10 minutes, then remove from the oven and allow to cool slightly.

9   Prepare the smoker for a 30-minute smoke session over low heat.

10 Place the mac 'n' cheeze pan in the smoker and smoked uncovered for 30 minutes. Remove from smoker and serve immediately.

SERVES 4

2 cups (300 g) raw cashews

16 ounces (455 g) large elbow noodles or other pasta

2 teaspoons granulated garlic

2 teaspoons granulated onion

½ teaspoon chili powder

½ teaspoon smoked paprika

2 teaspoons kosher salt

2 teaspoons yellow mustard

1 cup (65 g) nutritional yeast

3 cups (705 ml) unsweetened oat milk

1 tablespoon (15 g) unsalted vegan butter

½ cup (60 g) panko breadcrumbs

1 teaspoon dried thyme

2 cups (10 ounces) shredded vegan mozzarella

Smoked Feta Cheeze

An amazing "cheese" recipe that will go great with a nice pasta dish or on a great vegan cheese platter.

1 Put the almonds in a bowl and cover with hot, but not quite boiling, water. Soak for 1 hour, then drain and pat dry.

2 Combine the drained almonds, tofu, lemon juice, olive brine, white vinegar, 1 teaspoon of the salt, granulated onion, granulated garlic, and oregano in a food processor. Process until creamy, about 1 minute, stopping to scrape down the sides as needed.

3 Taste the mixture and add more lemon juice or salt, if desired. The flavors will become more muted; you want it to taste very tart and salty at this point. Run the processor again, until the consistency is fluffy, creamy, and only slightly textured. Add the agar powder, and pulse several times to incorporate.

4 Transfer the mixture to a small saucepan. Whisking constantly, cook over medium to medium-low heat until the cheese is steamy hot and thickened, 3 or 4 minutes. When you see bubbling and are certain the mixture has reached a boiling temperature, continue to whisk and cook for another 30 seconds.

5 Transfer the cheese to a ramekin or small container, and smooth the top. Allow to cool on the countertop for about 15 minutes, then cover with plastic wrap and refrigerate until cold, 2 to 3 hours. The flavor develops and improves overnight.

6 When you are ready to serve, simply scoop individual servings straight from the ramekin/mold, or run a butter knife around the edge, and turn the whole wheel of cheese onto a serving platter.

7 Once it's completely cooled, prep your smoker for a 15-minute smoke session over low heat. The feta will absorb flavors very easily.

8 Serve immediately. Store extra in an airtight container in the refrigerator for 5 to 7 days. It's also freezer-friendly (just make sure it is well-protected from air). Transfer the feta to the refrigerator to thaw overnight before serving.

SERVES 4

1 cup (110 g) blanched slivered almonds

7 ounces (200 g) extra-firm tofu, patted dry

¼ cup (60 ml) fresh lemon juice, plus more as needed

3 tablespoons (35 ml) brine from a jar of green olives

2 teaspoons white distilled or rice vinegar

1 to 1¼ teaspoons kosher salt

¼ teaspoon granulated onion

¼ teaspoon granulated garlic

Scant ¼ teaspoon dried oregano

2 teaspoons agar powder

Note

No-nut option: Substitute 1 cup (125 g) raw sunflower seeds for the almonds. Soak as instructed, then drain and briefly rinse under running water. Pat dry and proceed with the recipe as written.

Smoked Lobster Mushroom Mac 'n' Cheeze

This one's for my Boujee B*tches! When you wanna get fancy at the dinners, bring this one out! It's the ultimate family gathering dish that will have you the talk of the Instagram story.

SERVES 4

1 ounce (30 g) dried lobster mushrooms, covered with water and soaked overnight to rehydrate

1 cup (240 ml) cashew nut milk

2 tablespoons (30 ml) refined coconut oil

2 tablespoons (10 g) nutritional yeast

1 tablespoon (15 ml) mashed roasted garlic

2 tablespoons (30 ml) rice vinegar

1 tablespoon (15 g) white miso

1 tablespoon (15 ml) fresh lemon juice

Kosher salt

1 tablespoon (15 ml) vegetable oil

8 ounces (225 g) uncooked tubular pasta, such as cavatappi

3 shallots, thinly sliced

¼ cup (60 ml) strained mushroom soaking liquid

¾ cup (175 ml) water

2 tablespoons (15 g) dried breadcrumbs

1½ teaspoons vegetable oil

1 Squeeze the soaked mushrooms to release excess soaking liquid and place them on a strainer. Rinse the mushrooms to remove any grit. Cut into bite-size bits and set aside. Strain the mushroom-soaking liquid through kitchen paper and set aside.

2 To cook the macaroni, fill a big pot with salted water and bring to a boil. Cook according to the directions on the package (al dente). Drain the macaroni, reserving some of the water, and return into the same pot.

3 Combine the cashew milk, coconut oil, nutritional yeast, roasted garlic, rice wine vinegar, miso, and salt in a food processor. Process until smooth and creamy. If it becomes too thick, add a bit of the reserved pasta water and combine well.

4 Preheat the oven to 350°F (180°C). Put a 3-quart (3 L) baking dish on a half sheet pan.

5 Heat the tablespoon of oil in a cast-iron or nonstick pan. Once it starts bubbling, add the shallots and ¼ teaspoon of salt and sauté until translucent, about 5 minutes. Add the sliced mushrooms to the shallots and stir around. Add in the reserved mushroom liquid and water and allow to simmer. Simmer uncovered, whisking occasionally until the mushroom liquid has steamed off and the mushrooms are tender.

continued

6   Pour the shallot-mushroom mix and the prepared cheese sauce over the macaroni. Gently combine everything together with tongs. Add a bit of water if necessary to make the sauce nice and silky. Transfer the mixture into the baking dish.

7   In a separate small bowl mix, the breadcrumbs with the oil, working everything together until the oil is completely blended with the breadcrumbs. Sprinkle on top of the macaroni and cheese mixture.

8   Bake for 30 minutes, until the top is crunchy or golden brown. Let cool down for 10 minutes.

9   Finish this bad boy in your smoker for about 30 minutes at 165°–220°F (75°–105°C). Enjoy!

Drunken Beer Cheeze

Nothing like some boozie cheeze! This cheese sauce can be used for almost anything. Add a meat substitute to make it into the ultimate dip.

1 Whisk together the flour and oat milk in a medium saucepan until there are no clumps.

2 Whisk in the beer, nutritional yeast, vegan cream cheese, soy sauce, Dijon mustard, granulated garlic powder, smoked paprika, salt, and turmeric, if using. Heat over medium heat until the dip comes to a simmer. Simmer for 1 to 2 minutes, or until thickened. Taste and add more salt if needed. Serve warm.

SERVES 4

2 tablespoons (15 g) all-purpose flour

½ cup (120 ml) unsweetened oat milk

½ cup (120 ml) IPA beer (any brand will do)

¼ cup (15 g) nutritional yeast

8 ounces (225 g) vegan cream cheese, at room temperature

2 teaspoons soy sauce

1 teaspoon Dijon mustard

1 teaspoon granulated garlic

½ teaspoon smoked paprika

½ teaspoon kosher salt, plus more as needed

¼ teaspoon turmeric (optional, for color)

Smoky Fruits and Sweets

Grilled Fruit Skewers with Chile-Lime Glaze

You will need to soak 18 (6-inch/15 cm) bamboo skewers in water 20 minutes.

1 Thread the watermelon, pineapple, and mango cubes on the skewers. Put the skewers in a large zippered plastic bag, being careful not to puncture the bag; add the lime juice, seal, and toss gently to coat. Refrigerate at least 30 minutes, or until you are ready to smoke them.

2 Prepare the smoker for a 15-minute smoke (140°–165°F [60°–75°C]).

3 Remove the skewers from the bag and place on a baking sheet. Brush the fruit with vegetable oil and place the skewers on the grill of the smoker. Smoke for 15 minutes.

4 Transfer the fruit skewers to a serving platter. Combine the lime zest, chili powder, and 1 teaspoon salt in a small bowl. Sprinkle the seasoning over the fruit and serve.

SERVES 6

½ (5- to-6-pound/2.25 to 2.75 kg) seedless watermelon, cut into 1-inch (2.5 cm) cubes

1 pineapple, peeled, cored, and cut into 1-inch (2.5 cm) cubes

2 mangoes, peeled, pitted, and cut into 1-inch (2-cm) cubes

Grated zest and juice of 1 lime

Vegetable oil, for brushing

2 teaspoons chili powder

Coarse sea salt

Smoked Peaches with Vegan Rum Whip

In the South, especially where I'm from in Georgia, peaches are readily available. So here's another peachy recipe!

SERVES 4

4 peaches

1 tablespoon (15 g) raw sugar

1 cup (60 g) vegan whipped cream

2 teaspoons granulated white sugar

1 teaspoon vanilla extract

1 tablespoon (15 ml) spiced rum

1 Prepare the smoker for a 15-minute smoke (140°–165°F [60°–75°C]).

2 Halve the peaches and remove the stones. Freestone peaches will work the best in this recipe. Sprinkle the raw sugar evenly over the cut side of the peaches. Smoke them, cut side down, for 30 minutes.

3 Meanwhile, add the vegan whipped cream to a medium bowl and fold in the white sugar, vanilla, and rum.

4 Serve the warm peaches with a dollop of spiced rum whipped cream and enjoy!

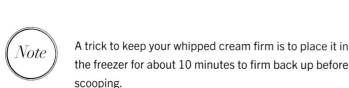

Note

A trick to keep your whipped cream firm is to place it in the freezer for about 10 minutes to firm back up before scooping.

Smoked Apple Pudding

Peaches are the best-known fruit for grilling and smoking, perhaps because their soft and porous flesh absorbs smoke well. Apples, I have found, soak up smoke flavor nearly as well—and taste better for it. Top the pudding with your favorite vegan ice cream or whipped cream.

SERVES 6

6 tart apples, peeled

¼ cup (30 g) all-purpose flour

1 cup (200 g) sugar

Pinch of kosher salt

About 2 cups (475 ml) unsweetened oat milk

1 Preheat the oven to 325°F (170°C). Also set the smoker for a 15-minute smoke (140°–165°F [60°–75°C]).

2 Place the apples directly onto the grill rack and smoke for 15 minutes.

3 Remove the apples from the smoker, core, cut into a medium dice.

4 Toss the apples with the flour, sugar, and salt and transfer into a 9 × 9-inch (23 × 23 cm) baking dish. Pour enough oat milk into dish to come almost to the top of the apples, but not cover them.

5 Bake for 45 minutes, until the apples are tender. Serve warm.

Note I tend to find that Granny Smith apples work best for baking, but any dense apple will work.

Smoked Boozy Pineapples

This summer gem is juicy and refreshing. Pair with vegan ice cream to make the ultimate tropical dessert.

1 To prepare the glaze, whisk together the rum, brown sugar, cinnamon, and vanilla in a 9 × 13-inch (23 × 33-cm) baking dish. Add the pineapple in a single layer and soak for at least 30 minutes, or even overnight.

2 Prepare the smoker for a 15-minute smoke session (140°–165°F [60°–75°C]). Line the grill racks with aluminum foil for easier clean up.

3 Place the pineapple on the grill racks. Smoke for 15 minutes.

4 Remove from the smoker and serve with ice cream.

SERVES 3 TO 4

1 cup (235 ml) rum

2 tablespoons (30 g) packed light brown sugar

2 teaspoons ground cinnamon

2 teaspoons vanilla extract

3 thick pineapple slices

Vegan vanilla ice cream

Smoked S'more Bananas

Kids love these campfire classics. They're fun and easy to make.

1 Prepare the smoker for a 15-minute smoke (140°–165°F [60°–75°C]).

2 Take a banana with its peel still on and cut down the middle (along the concave side) just until the tip of your knife just grazes the peel on the other side; do not cut all the way through. Pull the peel and banana slightly apart. Stuff with one-quarter of the chocolate and mini marshmallows (or other fillings, see notes below) into the center of the banana. Wrap the banana in foil. Repeat with the other bananas and filling.

3 Smoke for 15 minutes, or until the fillings have melted and the bananas have warmed through.

4 Unwrap the bananas and top with crushed graham cracker. Slice into halves. Enjoy.

SERVES 4

4 bananas

¼ cup (60 ml) shaved vegan milk chocolate

16 mini vegan marshmallows

2 graham cracker squares, crushed

Note You can always add ingredients, such as M&M's or other candies or crushed cookies.

Smoked Hot Mexican Chocolate

Man! This recipe is a surefire hit when the fall season rolls around. It has authentic Mexican chocolate flavors with just the right amount of kick.

1   Set the smoker temperature 180°F (80°C) and preheat with the lid closed for 15 minutes.

2   In a heatproof pan, smoke the cayenne pepper for approximately 30 minutes. Add the cinnamon and paprika to the pan and smoke for 5 more minutes.

3   Combine the milk, cream, and sugar in a medium saucepan and heat over low heat until scalded, 10 to 15 minutes. Whisk in the cocoa and salt. When the mixture is hot, stir in the chocolate, smoked spices, and vanilla. Whisk until combined.

4   Serve with whipped cream or marshmallows. Enjoy!

SERVES 4 TO 6

⅛ teaspoon cayenne pepper

½ teaspoon ground cinnamon

½ teaspoon smoked paprika

⅔ cup (160 ml) vegan cream

4 cups (940 ml) unsweetened oat milk

½ cup (100 g) sugar

¼ cup (45 g) cocoa powder

⅛ teaspoon kosher salt

2 tablespoons (30 ml) finely chopped bittersweet chocolate

½ teaspoon vanilla extract

Vegan whipped cream or marshmallows, to serve

Smoked Brandied Cherries

Peaches are the classic smoked fruit, but smoke-infused cherries are just as good.

SERVES 6 TO 8

½ cup (120 ml) water

½ cup (100 g) sugar

2 tablespoons (30 ml) fresh lemon juice

2 pounds (1 kg) sweet cherries, stemmed and pitted

1 to 1½ cups (235 to 355 ml) brandy

Diced lemon zest (optional)

1   Heat the water and sugar in a small saucepan, until the sugar completely dissolves. Transfer to a large bowl and set aside to cool. Add the lemon juice and stir to combine.

2   Prepare the smoker for a 10- to 15-minute smoke (140°–165°F [60°–75°C]).

3   Smoke the cherries for 10 to 15 minutes.

4   Transfer the smoked cherries into the large bowl with the lemon juice mixture. Add 1 cup (235 ml) of the brandy and gently stir to incorporate. Transfer the cherries into two clean pint (475 ml) mason jars. If needed, add brandy to cover the cherries, allowing for ½ inch (1 cm) headroom. Allow to cool thoroughly before adding the lids and securing the screwbands fingertight.

5   Refrigerate for 4 to 6 weeks before using in cocktails or desserts, with the diced lemon zest as garnish (optional).

8

Drinks

Distinguished Guest

The origins of the name of this drink are subject to debate, and they might well be lost to history. But there is no doubt that this is a very fine mocktail, garnished here, in the spirit of this book, with smoked cherries. The drink is a close cousin to the cocktail known as the Cape Codder.

Combine the cranberry juice, lime juice, and simple syrup in a shaker or a lidded jar and shake well. Pour into a coupe glass. Garnish with the cucumber slices and smoked cherries and serve.

SERVES 1

2 ounces (60 ml) cranberry juice

¾ ounce (20 ml) fresh lime juice

¾ ounce (20 ml) simple syrup

2 slices cucumber

5 Smoked Brandied Cherries (see recipe, page 188)

Mezcal Mule

Mezcal has a naturally smoky flavor, which makes it pair well with any kind of barbecue dinner. The Sombra brand is especially smoky and is widely available, but if you cannot find it you can use another mezcal.

Combine the lime slices and agave in a shaker and muddle. Add the mezcal and lime juice to a shaker filled with ice and shake until well-chilled. Strain into a rocks glass over fresh ice. Top with the ginger beer. Garnish with a cucumber slice and candied ginger and serve.

SERVES 1

3 slices lime

½ ounce (15 ml) agave syrup

1½ ounces (45 ml) mezcal (Sombra mezcal is recommended)

¾ ounce (20 ml) fresh lime juice

Ice

3 ounces (90 ml) ginger beer, plus more depending on the size of your glass, chilled

1 slice cucumber

1 piece candied ginger

Blackberry Paloma

*Tequila-and-fruit drinks make summer feel like summer,
and they go well alongside just about any kind of
barbecue, vegan included.*

1 Squeeze the juice from the lime quarter into a cocktail jigger.
 Gently muddle the blackberries, mint leaves, and squeezed lime
 quarter together. Add the cranberry juice, tequila, and agave.
 Shake until well mixed.

2 Fill a tall glass with crushed ice and pour the tequila mixture
 over. Top up with club soda. Garnish with mint and serve.

SERVES 1

¼ lime

5 fresh blackberries

2 fresh mint leaves, plus more
to garnish

½ cup (120 ml) cranberry juice

3 shots tequila

2 tablespoons (30 ml) agave
syrup

Crushed ice

½ cup (120 ml) club soda or
sparkling water

Smoked Peach Lemonade

We take our peaches very seriously in the southern United States where I live—especially in the summer, and often in refreshingly cold drinks like this one.

1   Combine the lemonade and peach slices in a blender. Blend until smooth. Pour into a large pitcher. Add the bourbon and liquid smoke, stirring to combine. Chill until you are ready to serve.

2   Fill glasses with ice and serve garnished with peach slices and thyme.

SERVES 4 TO 8

6 cups (1.4 L) lemonade, preferably made from freshly squeezed lemons

1 cup (170 g) peeled, ripe peach slices, plus more to garnish

1 cup (235 ml) bourbon

2 drops liquid smoke

Ice

Fresh thyme

Smoked Bloody Mary

If you like a good bloody Mary, you'll really love a smokin' good one.

1   Make the smoked ice: Prepare a smoker on low heat. Place 5 ice cubes in an aluminum pan in the smoker and smoke for 20 minutes. (Although they will of course melt into water, it is still better to start with cubes—for the smoke flavor will adhere better to the cubes than to liquid water.) Carefully remove the pan of water and pour it into an ice-cube tray. Freeze the smoked ice cubes.

2   Mix or shake together the V8 juice, vodka, 1 ounce (30 ml) of the VBQ sauce, lime juice, pickle juice, Worcestershire sauce, horseradish, hot sauce, salt, and pepper in a cocktail shaker or medium jar.

3   Pour the remaining teaspoon of VBQ Sauce into a small plate or saucer and spread it out evenly. Take a lime wedge and run it around the rim of a tall (highball) glass to moisten it the rim of the glass. Invert the glass and place it on the spice mix and twist it until the rim is well coated.

4   Add the add the smoked ice cubes to the glass, pour the drink over the rocks, and hang the lime wedge on the lip of the glass. Serve immediately.

SERVES 1

5 cubes smoked ice (directions below, in step 1)

4 ounces (120 ml) V8 juice

1½ ounces (44 ml) 80 proof unflavored vodka

1 ounce plus 1 teaspoon (35 ml) Smoky Vidalia VBQ Sauce (see recipe, page 38)

1 tablespoon (15 ml) fresh lime juice

1 teaspoon dill pickle juice

½ teaspoon Worcestershire sauce

⅛ teaspoon bottled horseradish in vinegar (not creamy horseradish)

1 or 2 squirts of bottled hot sauce with chipotles, such as Tabasco Chipotle sauce

¼ teaspoon coarse Kosher salt

2 pinches black pepper

Lime wedges and olives, for garnish

5 cubes smoked ice

Cloudy Tokyo

Barbecue culture has legions of drinks, such as this Asian-inspired alcohol-free mocktail, where liquid smoke gives the entire drink a sultry, smoky flavor. This is one of my favorites.

Combine the tea, coconut milk, and liquid smoke in a tall highball glass or other glass and stir. Pour the chilled soda over the mixture and serve.

SERVES 1

5 ounces (150 ml) green tea, chilled

½ ounce (15 ml) unsweetened coconut milk

1 drop liquid smoke

5 ounces (150 ml) coconut soda, chilled

Terry Sargent *is the foremost authority on vegan barbecue in the U.S. A native of Georgia, he was* Southern Living *magazine's 2021 "Cook of the Year." Terry worked for twenty years, from his mid-teens to his mid-thirties, as a chef in Atlanta, during which time he was a devoted carnivore. When his doctor told him he was facing some significant health risks, he quit his corporate-chef gig and learned everything he could about plant-based foods and cooking. Starting in 2017, he began running vegan BBQ pop-up restaurants around Atlanta; their success eventually led him to open a standalone restaurant, Grass VBQ Joint, one of the first vegan barbecue restaurants in the world. He has been featured in the* Washington Post, *Thrillist, Eater, VegNews, and many other outlets. He lives in the Atlanta area.*

Index

Note: Page references in *italics* indicate photographs.